CONTEMPORARY ISSUES

IMMIGRATION

CONTEMPORARY ISSUES

CRIMINAL JUSTICE SYSTEM
EDUCATION
THE ENVIRONMENT
GENDER EQUALITY
GUN CONTROL
HEALTH CARE
IMMIGRATION
JOBS AND ECONOMY
MENTAL HEALTH
POVERTY AND WELFARE
PRIVACY AND SOCIAL MEDIA
RACE RELATIONS
RELIGIOUS FREEDOM

CONTEMPORARY ISSUES

IMMIGRATION

HEATHER PIDCOCK-REED

MASON CREST
PHILADELPHIA | MIAMI

MASON CREST
450 Parkway Drive, Suite D, Broomall, Pennsylvania 19008
(866) MCP-BOOK (toll-free) • www.masoncrest.com

Printed and bound in the United States of America.

CPSIA Compliance Information: Batch #CCRI2019.
For further information, contact Mason Crest at 1-866-MCP-Book.

First printing
1 3 5 7 9 8 6 4 2

ISBN (hardback) 978-1-4222-4394-7
ISBN (series) 978-1-4222-4387-9
ISBN (ebook) 978-1-4222-7409-5

Library of Congress Cataloging-in-Publication Data
on file at the Library of Congress

Interior and cover design: Torque Advertising + Design
Production: Michelle Luke

Publisher's Note: Websites listed in this book were active at the time of publication. The publisher is not responsible for websites that have changed their address or discontinued operation since the date of publication. The publisher reviews and updates the websites each time the book is reprinted.

QR CODES AND LINKS TO THIRD-PARTY CONTENT

You may gain access to certain third-party content ("Third-Party Sites") by scanning and using the QR Codes that appear in this publication (the "QR Codes"). We do not operate or control in any respect any information, products, or services on such Third-Party Sites linked to by us via the QR Codes included in this publication, and we assume no responsibility for any materials you may access using the QR Codes. Your use of the QR Codes may be subject to terms, limitations, or restrictions set forth in the applicable terms of use or otherwise established by the owners of the Third-Party Sites. Our linking to such Third-Party Sites via the QR Codes does not imply an endorsement or sponsorship of such Third-Party Sites or the information, products, or services offered on or through the Third-Party Sites, nor does it imply an endorsement or sponsorship of this publication by the owners of such Third-Party Sites.

CONTENTS

KEY ICONS TO LOOK FOR:

Words to Understand: These words with their easy-to-understand definitions will increase the reader's understanding of the text while building vocabulary skills.

Sidebars: This boxed material within the main text allows readers to build knowledge, gain insights, explore possibilities, and broaden their perspectives by weaving together additional information to provide realistic and holistic perspectives.

Educational videos: Readers can view videos by scanning our QR codes, providing them with additional educational content to supplement the text. Examples include news coverage, moments in history, speeches, iconic sports moments, and much more!

Text-Dependent Questions: These questions send the reader back to the text for more careful attention to the evidence presented there.

Research Projects: Readers are pointed toward areas of further inquiry connected to each chapter. Suggestions are provided for projects that encourage deeper research and analysis.

Series Glossary of Key Terms: This back-of-the-book glossary contains terminology used throughout this series. Words found here increase the reader's ability to read and comprehend higher-level books and articles in this field.

WORDS TO UNDERSTAND

indentured servants—a person who has signed a contract to work for an employer until a pre-determined amount of time has passed, after which the indentured servant is granted freedom.

Industrial Revolution—the period of time during the late 1700s to early 1800s that saw many changes in manufacturing and industry.

Gilded Age—the period of time between the American Civil War and World War I that led to an expansion of the population of the United States; also known as a period of greed and corruption in which wealthy Americans lived materialistic lives.

resident alien—a person who is a citizen of a foreign country who lives in a country where they are not a citizen.

refugees—people who involuntarily leave their home countries due to war, persecution, or natural disaster.

A HISTORY AND OVERVIEW OF IMMIGRATION

Located on a plaque that is affixed to the Statue of Liberty on Ellis Island in New York City is a sonnet composed by Emma Lazarus in 1883. This sonnet is entitled "The New Colossus." It reads:

> Not like the brazen giant of Greek fame,
> With conquering limbs astride from land to land;
> Here at our sea-washed, sunset gates shall stand
> A mighty woman with a torch, whose flame
> Is the imprisoned lightning, and her name
> Mother of Exiles. From her beacon-hand
> Glows world-wide welcome; her mild eyes command
> The air-bridged harbor that twin cities frame.
> "Keep, ancient lands, your storied pomp!" cries she
> With silent lips. "Give me your tired, your poor,
> Your huddled masses yearning to breathe free,
> The wretched refuse of your teeming shore.
> Send these, the homeless, tempest-tossed to me,
> I lift my lamp beside the golden door!"[1]

The last lines of this sonnet have become a part of American culture. For many people, it represents the ideals that make America a great country. Those ideals are ones of a free country that welcomes everyone to come and make a life for himself or herself, no matter where they are from. They are the same ideals that make the United States a place of refuge for many immigrants who come from war-torn or poverty stricken countries in order to have better lives.

America has long been known as a melting pot of different cultures and peoples. Emma Lazarus' poem fully embraces that viewpoint of America. Many other poets, novelists, playwrights, and other artists have also embraced this

Immigrants wave as their boat passes the Statue of Liberty on the way to the Ellis Island Immigration Station, 1950s.

view of America. In a 1908 play called *The Melting Pot*, the protagonist of the play states, "Understand that America is God's Crucible, the great Melting-Pot where all the races of Europe are melting and re-forming! Here you stand, good folk, think I, when I see them at Ellis Island, here you stand in your fifty groups, your fifty languages, and histories, and your fifty blood hatreds and rivalries. But you won't be long like that, brothers, for those are the fires of God you've come to—these are the fires of God...into the Crucible with you all! God is making the American."[2]

This attitude of welcome to immigrants who are willing to become a part of the fabric of the American story is one that has persisted throughout the history of the United States. However, alongside this welcome is also a strand of hostility that has been directed towards various immigrant groups. While attention has shifted over time to groups from different areas, many of the same issues behind that hostility are still present today. In order to shed some light on these current issues, a brief history of immigration within the United States follows.

IMMIGRATION TO THE COLONIES

Colonists from Europe initially settled the United States. These early settlers came primary from Spain, France, England, Sweden, and the Netherlands. While many of these settlers came of their own free will, others were not as lucky. Some of the early colonists also brought slaves with them. These slaves came from Africa and the Caribbe-

During the seventeenth and eighteenth centuries, many people came to North America seeking religious freedom. One of these groups was the Pilgrims, who in 1620 established the Plymouth Colony in present-day Massachusetts.

an. This means that slavery was a part of the fabric of the North American colonial life from the year 1619. In addition to slaves, **indentured servants** were brought to the colonies. There were even convicts who were sent to the United States as a part of their sentence.

By the middle of the 1700s, the British colonies had proven to be the most successful colonies. During this time period there were so many English citizens migrating to the colonies that the English Parliament briefly to considered a total ban on allowing British citizens to immigrate to the colonies.

During the lead-up to the American Revolution, many of the colonists began to think about the role that the colonies played in providing refuge to those wishing to escape conditions in their home countries. In 1776, Thomas Paine published "Common Sense." In this pamphlet, he argued the case for the colonists to become independent of England. Paine writes, "Europe, and not England, is the parent country of America. This new world hath been the

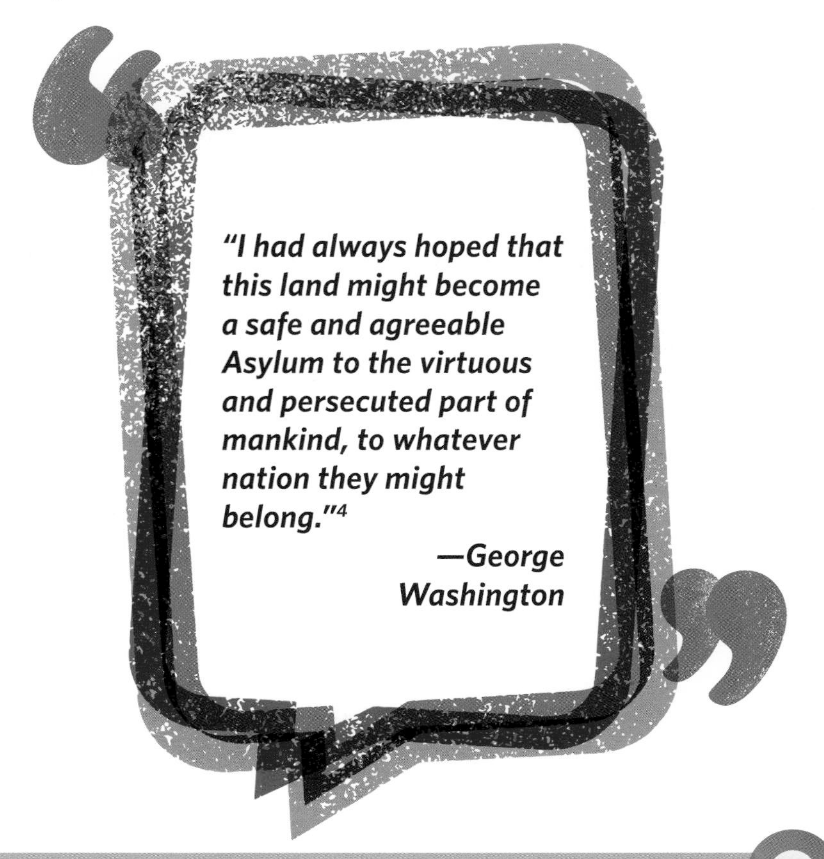

Millions of immigrants had no choice in the matter. Between 1619 and 1808, many Africans were brought to the American colonies forcibly as slaves.

asylum for the persecuted lovers of civil and religious liberty from every part of Europe."[3]

IMMIGRATION TO A NEW COUNTRY

After the American Revolution came to an end in 1783, the newly formed United States government decided to conduct the first Census of the population. The Census found that "of the 3.9 million people counted, the English were the largest ethnic group. Nearly 20 percent were of African heritage. German, Scottish, and Irish residents were also well represented."[5] The very first Naturalization Act was passed in the year 1790. This act stipulated that any immigrant who was a free white person could come to the United States and become a citizen.

At first, the immigration rate was rather low. An estimated 6,000 people entered the United States per year in the late eighteenth century and the early years of the nineteenth century. The number dropped even lower during the War of 1812 that took place between Great Britain and the United States. Once that war ended, however, the United States began to see larger number of immigrants enter the country. Most of these immigrants came from Great Britain, Ireland, and Western Europe.

The beginnings of the **Industrial Revolution** saw even more immigrants arriving at the shores of the United States. During the 1840s and 1850s, the majority of these immigrants came from Ireland to escape a terrible potato famine. Nearly 1.5 million Irish citizens made their way to America during this time period. The influx of immigrants, however, caused some negative feelings from native-born Americans. Irish immigrants, along with immigrants from Asia, were accused of stealing jobs from "real" Americans. It was during this time period that the Know Nothing party was

THE KNOW NOTHINGS

Political parties running on anti-immigrant platforms are not a modern phenomenon. In the 1850s, a political party known as the American Party, but commonly referred to as the Know Nothing Party, was formed. This party "strongly opposed immigrants and followers of the Catholic Church.... The Know Nothing Party intended to prevent Catholics and immigrants from being elected to political offices. Its members also hoped to deny these people jobs in the private sector, arguing that the nation's business owners needed to employ true Americans."[6]

In addition to being afraid that immigrants were taking jobs from American citizens, the Know Nothings were also afraid that Roman Catholics would take over the country and place it under the rule of the Pope. While these fears were totally unfounded, they certainly felt valid to the white, working-class Protestants who supported the Know Nothing Party.

formed. This political party was both anti-immigrant and anti-Catholic. (Most of the Irish were Roman Catholics, at a time that most Americans were Protestant Christians.)

IMMIGRATION IN THE GOLDEN AGE OF IMMIGRATION

The end of the Civil War ushered in the period of time that is known as the **Gilded Age**. This period sometimes referred to as the "Golden Age of Immigration." In the years between 1880 and 1930, over 27 million people entered the

Christopher Phillips, a professor of history at the University of Cincinnati states that the Know Nothings show patterns that are common to every nativist movements, even those present in today's political landscape. "First is the embrace of nationalism....Second is religious discrimination: in this case, Protestants against Catholics rather than the more modern day squaring-off of Judeo-Christians against Muslims. Lastly, a working-class identity exerts itself in conjunction with the rhetoric of upper-class political leaders."[7]

While the Know Nothing movement garnered a great deal of support, it ultimately collapsed due to its inability to take a position over the topic of slavery—the most controversial issue in the period leading up to the American Civil War. While the Know Nothing Party withered away in the late 1850s, the nativist spirit that once drove it has persisted.

An immigrant family arrives from Europe, 1907. They are walking with their belongings up the path to the Ellis Island Immigration Station, where they will be processed for entry into the United States.

United States. Many of these immigrants were from southern or eastern Europe and included many Italians and Jews. This influx of immigration was primarily driven by the Industrial Revolution.

While those of European descent were accepted (reluctantly in some cases), immigrants of other nationalities were outright despised. In response to an influx in Chinese immigrants to the west coast, who worked on railroads and in the mining industry, the Chinese Exclusion Act was passed in 1882. This act banned Chinese workers from coming into America, as they were seen as a threat to American jobs. Nearly a decade later, the Immigration Act of 1891 was passed. This piece of legislation banned immigrants who were sick, convicted of certain crimes, or polygamists.

Even though restrictions on immigration were beginning to be placed on certain groups, the United States opened up Ellis Island in 1892. This was the first official immigration station in America. Before the station closed in 1954, more than 12 million immigrants would pass through the gates at Ellis Island on their way to becoming citizens of the United States.

Scan here to watch a short video on Ellis Island.

This 1921 cartoon shows Uncle Sam imposing a 3 percent quota to reduce the flow of immigrants into the United States. The quota system began after the First World War and lasted until the 1960s.

IMMIGRATION AFTER THE GOLDEN AGE

The Golden Age of Immigration came to an end during World War I. The conflict in Europe caused a great many Americans to view foreigners suspiciously. Once the war had ended, a number of legislative acts were passed that limited the number of immigrants who would be allowed into the United States. The Great Depression of the 1930s further reduced the flow of immigrants into the country.

At the outbreak of World War II, immigrants from Italy, Germany, and Japan were treated with suspicion. After the Japanese surprise attack on Pearl Harbor in December 1941, many Japanese **resident aliens** and citizens of Japanese descent were placed into internment camps.

Things began to change after the end of World War II, when the US Congress passed the Displaced Persons Act of 1948. This law allowed entry to many **refugees** who were left homeless after the war. President Harry S. Truman, who said of the refugee crisis, "I urge the Congress to turn its attention to this world problem in an effort to find ways whereby we can fulfill our responsibilities to these thousands of homeless and suffering refugees of all faiths,"[8] prompted the passage of this legislation.

Beginning in 1956, the United States began to admit several thousand refugees from the Cold War. By the end of this showdown with the Soviet Union, the United States would allow over 3 million people into the country. By the time the 1960s arrived, American citizens were calling for more immigration reform.

The Immigration and Naturalization Act of 1965 was passed in response to growing concerns surrounding immigration. The new legislation eliminated restrictions on immigration from certain parts of the world. It did not, however, allow for any large increase in immigration. Only 170,000 people would be allowed to enter from the Eastern Hemisphere and 120,000 from the Western. Exceptions could be made, however, for relatives of individuals already in the United States and for refugees escaping political oppression or war.

This resulted in a huge change in the pattern of immigration to America. Newcomers were more often from Asia than from Europe. The war in Vietnam and the spread of Communism contributed to this trend. Most of the hundreds of thousands of refugees seeking asylum in America were Vietnamese, Chinese, Cambodians, and Laotians. Many Japanese, Filipinos, and Koreans also arrived.

However, after 1965 the largest number of immigrants came from Mexico. Mexican immigration posed unique challenges to American officials. Until the mid-nineteenth century much of the southwestern United States had been Mexican territory, and many families had relatives living on both sides of the border. In addition, Mexican farm workers had traditionally crossed the border to work in the United States, often for months at a time, then returned home to their families.

After the 1965 Immigration Act, millions of Mexicans became legal immigrants to the United States, but many

"I received a letter just before I left office from a man. I don't why he chose to write it, but I'm glad he did. He wrote that you can go to live in France, but you can't become a Frenchman. You can go to live in Germany or Italy, but you can't become a German, an Italian. He went through Turkey, Greece, Japan, and other countries. But he said anyone, from any corner of the world, can come to live in the United States and become an American."[9]

— Ronald Reagan

others crossed the border without proper documentation to live and work in the United States illegally. By 1980, nearly one million Mexican migrants were being caught trying to sneak across the border every year.

The Immigration Reform and Control Act of 1986, signed by President Ronald Reagan, was intended to deal with the growing problem of illegal immigration. The legislation created a path towards citizenship for approximately 3 million illegal immigrants living in America. It was supposed to prevent future illegal immigration by increasing border patrols and enforcing immigration regulations.

The clauses in the 1965 Immigration Act that allowed exceptions for family members and refugees made the United States a major immigrant-accepting nation again. By the 1980s and 1990s, America was welcoming near-record numbers of immigrants—sometimes more than half a million new immigrants every year.

IMMIGRATION IN TODAY'S AMERICA

Today, there are an estimated 60 million immigrants or children of immigrants residing within the United States. According to data compiled by the Pew Research Center, the majority of immigrants to America come from Mexico. While the majority of these immigrants are here legally, there are also an estimated 11 million illegal immigrants living in the United States. This has caused an uptick in the amount of concern over illegal immigration. Solutions to the problem have ranged from building a border wall to mass deportations to allowing some form of citizenship to otherwise law-abiding undocumented immigrants.

While there have been a number of politicians who ran campaigns based on anti-immigrant sentiments, the election of Donald J. Trump to the presidency in 2016 caused many immigrants to begin to feel uncertain as to their place in America. His insistence on building a border wall between Mexico and the United States, as well as his administration's proposals to restrict immigration and to ban immigrants who have utilized public assistance from being granted citizenship, have brought many of the old debates

New Yorkers protest against proposed immigration restrictions, including the expansion of a wall along the southern border of the United States, 2017.

concerning immigration back to the forefront of the American public.

The issues surrounding immigration are largely the same as they have been throughout the history of the United States. Many Americans are worried about the impact that immigrants have on the job market. According to Professor Charles Hirschman, "With globalization and massive industrial restructuring dominating many traditional sources of employment (both blue-collar and white-collar), many native-born citizens are fearful about their (and their children's future."[10]

Hirschman also points out that, "Many Americans, like people everywhere, are more comfortable with the familiar than with change. They fear that newcomers with different languages, religions, and cultures are reluctant to assimilate into American society and to learn English."[11] While these fears are not new, it is important that Americans become educated on the issues surrounding immigration so that they can understand and learn to accept the place of immigration within the American psyche.

TEXT-DEPENDENT QUESTIONS

1. In the first American Census, what nationality comprised the majority of citizens in the United States?
2. Why did the Know Nothing Party oppose Catholics and immigrants?
3. How many immigrants came to the United States through Ellis Island?
4. What is the name of the sonnet by Emma Lazarus that is attached to the Statue of Liberty?

RESEARCH PROJECTS

Conduct your own research on the Know Nothing Party and on modern anti-immigrant political platforms. Based on your research, write a two-page paper comparing and contrasting the Know Nothing Party and modern arguments against immigration. Remember to cite reputable sources within your paper.

WORDS TO UNDERSTAND

visas—documents granted to foreign nationals who wish to legally move to the United States and typically based on employment, student or familial status.

national security—the security of a country.

national identity—a sense of belonging to a particular country or nation, encompassing traditions, language and culture.

constituents—members of an electing group, for instance, those who have voted a person into a political office.

low-skilled occupations—jobs or careers that are attainable for those who have no form of higher education or highly developed job skills.

CHAPTER 2

SHOULD LEGAL IMMIGRATION TO THE UNITED STATES BE RESTRICTED?

Since the 2016 presidential election, advocates for the rights of immigrants have been concerned over potential changes to immigrant policies in the United States. President Trump and some of the members of his administration have expressed their desires to cut back on the number of immigrants legally permitted to enter the United States each year. "The American people were warned—let me [be] sarcastic when I remark on that—[they] were quote-unquote warned by Hillary Clinton that if they elected Donald Trump, he would enforce an extremely tough immigration policy, crack down on illegal immigration, deport people who were here illegally, improve our vetting and screening, and all these other things. And many people replied to that by voting for Donald Trump,"[14] Stephen Miller, one of Trump's senior advisors and a long-time advocate of immigration restrictions, said.

According to the Pew Research Center, there are 43.7 million foreign-born people residing in the United States, with the majority of these immigrants (76 percent) being here legally. Each year, approximately a million immigrants arrive in the United States. The number of immigrants arriving to this country every year has been hotly contested in the political arena for many years.

The debates surrounding legal immigration have been occurring since before the United States was its own country. In 1751, Benjamin Franklin wrote, "The importation of foreigners into a country that has an many inhabitants as the present employments and provisions for subsistence will bear, will be in the end no increase of people, unless the new comers have more industry and frugality than the natives, and then they will provide more subsistence, and increase in the country; but they will gradually eat the natives out. Nor is it necessary to bring in foreigners to fill up any occasional vacancy in a country for such vacancy will soon be filled by natural generation."[13]

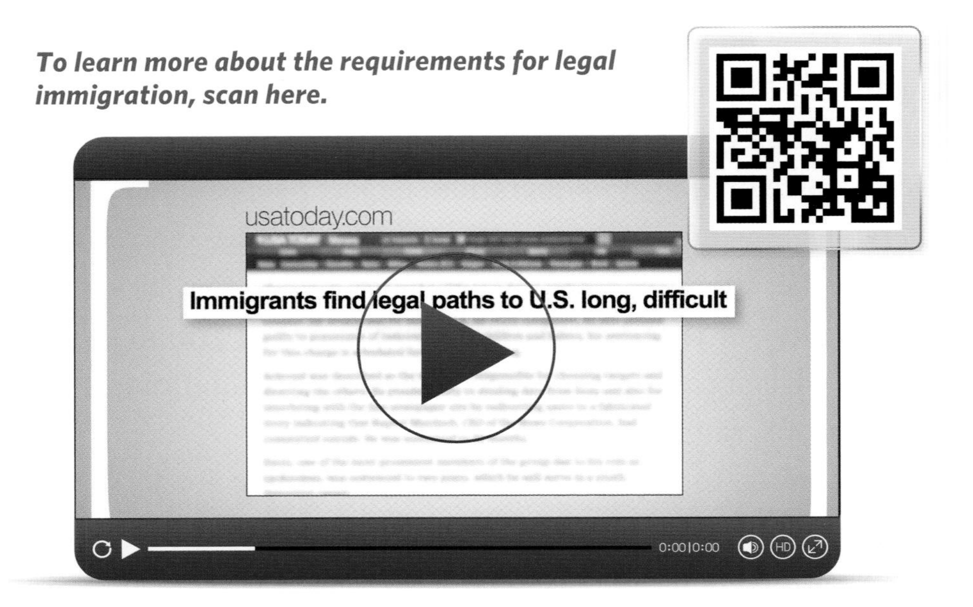

To learn more about the requirements for legal immigration, scan here.

Application to Register Permanent Residence or Adjust Status

Department of Homeland Security
U.S. Citizenship and Immigration Services

USCIS
Form I-485
OMB No. 1615-0023
Expires 06/30/2019

For USCIS Use Only

	Receipt	Action Block
Preference Category:		
Country Chargeable:		
Priority Date:		
Date Form I-693 Received:		
☐ Applicant Interviewed ☐ Interview Waived Date of Initial Interview: ______ Lawful Permanent Resident as of: ______	**Section of Law** ☐ INA 209(a) ☐ INA 249 ☐ INA 209(b) ☐ Sec. 13, Act of 9/11/57 ☐ INA 245(a) ☐ Cuban Adjustment Act ☐ INA 245(i) ☐ Other ______ ☐ INA 245(m)	

To be completed by an attorney or accredited representative (if any).

☐ **Select this box if Form G-28 is attached.**	**Volag Number** (if any)	**Attorney State Bar Number** (if applicable)	**Attorney or Accredited Representative USCIS Online Account Number** (if any)

► **START HERE - Type or print in black ink.** A-Number ► **A-**

NOTE TO ALL APPLICANTS: If you do not completely fill out this application or fail to submit required documents listed in the Instructions, U.S. Citizenship and Immigration Services (USCIS) may deny your application.

Part 1. Information About You (Person applying for lawful permanent residence)

Your Current Legal Name *(do not provide a nickname)*

1.a. Family Name (Last Name)
1.b. Given Name (First Name)
1.c. Middle Name

Other Names You Have Used Since Birth *(if applicable)*

NOTE: Provide all other names you have ever used, including your family name at birth, other legal names, nicknames, aliases, and assumed names. If you need extra space to complete this section, use the space provided in **Part 14. Additional Information**.

2.a. Family Name (Last Name)
2.b. Given Name

3.a. Family Name (Last Name)
3.b. Given Name (First Name)
3.c. Middle Name

4.a. Family Name (Last Name)
4.b. Given Name (First Name)
4.c. Middle Name

Other Information About You

5. Date of Birth (mm/dd/yyyy)

NOTE: In addition to providing your actual date of birth, include any other dates of birth you have used in connection with any legal names or non-legal names in the space provided in **Part 14. Additional Information**.

6. Sex ☐ Male ☐ Female
7. City or Town of Birth

Foreign nationals who want to live and work in the United States must apply for permanent resident status using form I-485.

Thomas Jefferson, another founding father and the third president of the United States, was in favor of legal immigration while writing to a potential immigrant to the newly formed country, "Born in other countries, yet believ-

TRUMP'S PROPOSED RESTRICTIONS

The administration of President Trump has proposed a number of policies on legal immigration that have proven to be controversial. Many of these policies have been challenged in the courts, some even making their way up to the Supreme Court. While some of the policies have to do with illegal immigrants and the children of these immigrants, others have impacted both asylum seekers and other legal immigrants.

One of the more controversial policies enacted by the administration is a proposed "Muslim ban." This policy banned immigrants from seven countries that hold Muslim-majority populations under the argument that keeping these people out would help to prevent terrorist attacks on United States soil. Foreign nationals seeking to come to the United States from Iran, Libya, Somalia, Yemen, Sudan, Iraq, and Syria were impacted by this policy. Protests and legal challenges to the policy caused it to be revised several times. The Supreme Court of the United States eventually upheld the third version of the policy.

ing you could be happy in this, our laws acknowledge, as they should do, your right to join us in society, conforming, as I doubt not you will do, to our established rules."[14]

This clash in viewpoints carries on into modern times. According to a 2015 study conducted by the Pew Research Center, 49 percent of Americans stated that legal immigration rates should be decreased, while 34 percent of Americans thought that the number of legal immigrants

Another policy enacted by the Trump administration cut the number of refugees permitted into the United States in half, to 50,000. This makes it more difficult for those seeking asylum to enter legally.

In September 2018, a new proposal was brought forth that would deny permanent resident cards (also known as "green cards") to any immigrant who had previously received government assistance such as food stamps, Medicaid, or housing vouchers. While this proposal has not yet been enacted, it has caused a significant outcry from anti-poverty and pro-immigration groups, as it would not only make life harder for many immigrants already here, but it could also deter low-income families from deciding to come to the United States at all.

It remains to be seen what the long-term effects of many of these policies and proposals would be. However, the Trump administration's significant departure from the immigrant policies of President Barack Obama shows just how the scenario for immigrants in the United States is constantly changing.

admitted to the United States should remain the same. Only 15 percent of Americans were in favor of increasing the number of immigrants allowed into the country. While opinions on the numbers of immigrants allowed into the country are divided, the majority of Americans (65 percent) believe that immigrants make the United States a stronger country, with only 26 percent saying that immigrants are a burden on the United States.

The debate over legal immigration in the United States and whether or not it should be restricted continues on. The following essays explore both sides of the issue.

An example of a green card, carried by legal immigrants to show that they are permitted to live and work in the United States.

LEGAL IMMIGRATION TO THE UNITED STATES SHOULD BE RESTRICTED

The election of Donald Trump to the Presidency of the United States brought an administration into the White House that has "granted fewer **visas**, approved fewer refugees, ordered the removal of hundreds of thousands of legal residents whose home countries have been hit by war and natural disaster, and pushed Congress to pass laws to dramatically cut the entire legal immigration system."[15]

Trump's hardline stance on immigration is one of the reasons why he was elected and many of his and his administration's position echo that of the nearly half of Americans who indicated that immigration rates should be restricted. There are a number of reasons why legal immigration to the United States should be limited.

One of the primary reasons why legal immigration should have restrictions placed on it is that immigrant populations can use up a large number of both government and community resources. A report published by the Urban Institute in 2017 states that "if the costs of government spending, including public goods, are allocated to all people equally, immigrant adults are costlier to state and local budgets than native adults, with almost $3,000 more spent per adult."[16] When large groups of immigrants move into an area, they tend to utilize services like food banks, food stamps, healthcare services, and housing. This can cause stress on these local resources, making them more difficult for citizens to use them and making some of these services

"Restricted immigration is not an offensive but purely a defensive action. It is not adopted in criticism of others in the slightest degree, but solely for the purpose of protecting ourselves. We cast no aspersions on any race or creed, but we must remember that every object of our institutions of society and government will fail unless America be kept American."[17]

—Calvin Coolidge, thirtieth president of the United States

more costly to operate. In addition, immigrants are more likely to have more dependent children than the average American citizen. These children are often in need of extra educational resources, making them more costly on the education system as well.

National security is another concern when it comes to the number of immigrants who are permitted to legally enter the country. In an era when terrorism against the United States is a top concern, many people wish to ensure that immigrants to this country are properly vetted. Even with this vetting, there could possibly be a risk to the security of the United States. For instance, all nineteen of the terrorists responsible for the attacks of September 11, 2001 had entered the country legally. At the time of the attacks, seventeen were still carrying valid United States visas. “Foreign-born militant Islamic terrorists have used almost every conceivable means of entering the country,” explains Steven A. Camarota, director of research at the Center for Immigration Studies (CIS). “They have come as students, tourists, and business visitors. They have also been Lawful Permanent Residents (LPRs) and naturalized US citizens....

Communities with large immigrant populations tend to spend more on schools because of the demand for English as a Second Language classes and other special services.

Terrorists have even used America's humanitarian tradition of welcoming those seeking asylum."[18]

A restriction in the number of immigrants allowed into the United States also ensures that jobs are not taken away from American citizens who need them. While there isn't any one career field or type of job that contains more immigrants than native-born workers, there are some

Americans with no education beyond high school are most likely to be impacted by the arrival of immigrant workers. Both immigrants and high school graduates or dropouts often compete for the same types of labor-intensive jobs.

fields where a large percentage of the workers are immigrants. In some jobs (such as construction, farm labor, housekeeping and other jobs that don't require education beyond high school), immigrants will accept lower wages than native-born Americans will. This can impact a significant portion of the American workforce in a negative way. By restricting the number of low-skill immigrants into the country, and therefore preventing them from entering the workforce, allowing for improvements in the employment rate for native-born citizens, as well as leading to improvements in working conditions across the board. For instance, in cases where immigrant labor becomes unavailable higher wages, better benefits, and safer workplace practices become the norm, opening up interest from American-born workers. A good example of this is a poultry plant in Georgia that lost a significant portion of its workforce due to an immigration raid. To address the shortage, "the plant immediately advertised higher wages, free transportation, and on-site housing."[19]

In addition to reducing the number of jobs available to native-born Americans, immigration can also have a negative impact on the **national identity** and culture of the United States. Many areas with a large proportion of immigrant groups find that the immigrants who move into the area do not fully assimilate. This can lead to a number of immigrants who do not have deep ties of loyalty to the United States or who have no wish to adopt and preserve the cultural identity of the area in which they have moved.

While the United States is often known as a "melting pot" of different cultures, it is important to understand that "the very concept of a nation is a form of social identity that unites people into national groups."[20] A failure to fully assimilate into the surrounding area and to fully identify as an American can lead to a lack of cohesion within communities and the United States as a whole.

Another reason why legal immigration should be heavily restricted is that it can have a negative impact on the immigrant's home country. Immigrants admitted to the United States are often some of the best workers, innovators, and thinkers in their home countries. By admitting these workers into the United States, our country indirectly contributes to the decline or the lack of improvement within their own countries. Keeping immigration rates low within the United States will allow these immigrants to work on improving the economy, living conditions and cultural environment of their own home countries.

As the discussion over the number of legal immigrants admitted each year continues, it is important to understand that we must protect the interests of American citizens over those of foreigners who want to come to our country. Limiting the number of immigrants allowed into our country allows us to focus on keeping the United States secure and economically viable.

To enter the United States legally, immigrants must present themselves at ports of entry, such as this one on the US-Mexico border at El Paso, Texas. There, federal officers can inspect the immigrant's visa and ensure that the person has been approved for entry.

An immigrant receives a certificate of American citizenship during a naturalization ceremony in Boston. Naturalization is the process through which immigrants gain the full benefits of citizenship, including the right to vote and to hold public office.

LEGAL IMMIGRATION TO THE UNITED STATES SHOULD NOT BE RESTRICTED

In a letter written to a **constituent**, Dick Armey, a former United States Representative from the state of Texas, wrote,

> In my view, immigrants today aren't any different from immigrants who have come to America throughout our nation's history. They bring new ideas, an entrepreneurial spirit and close family ties. They place a high value on education. And they are eager to achieve the American Dream....It's to our benefit to keep our doors open, and to keep enriching our economy and culture. I'd like to see America continue to do so.[21]

Representative Armey's opinion reflects a bipartisan attitude that has long been present within American politics. This is a belief is that legal immigration to the United States should be encouraged, as it is a good thing economically, culturally, and socially for our country.

One of the primary arguments in favor of not restricting immigration to the United States is that immigration is good for the economy. Legal immigrants come to the United States in order to better their lives. This means that some of the brightest and ambitious people wish to come to the United States. Their drive, hard work, and innovation make America's economy stronger. In fact, recent studies show that, "Despite making up only 14 percent of the US population, migrants have founded 40 percent of businesses on the Fortune 500, and about 30 percent of all the country's businesses since 2011, including more than half of the startup businesses now valued at over

"Immigration benefits the US. The economic advantages are significant. Many immigrants are natural entrepreneurs, establishing companies, creating jobs, and driving innovation. Well-educated and highly trained foreign workers are inventive and productive. Expanded work forces increase business flexibility, allowing companies to quickly respond to changing demands."[22]

—Doug Bandow, Senior Fellow at the Cato Institute

$1 billion."[23] Ian Goldin, a professor at Oxford University writes in the study that, "Their presence usually is associated with higher wages, higher productivity, lower unemployment and higher female workforce participation."[24]

Going hand in hand with the favorable impact on the United States economy is the fact that immigrants often perform low-paying jobs that natural born American citizens find to be undesirable. These include jobs in agriculture, construction, buildings and grounds maintenance, and other industries. Since many of these **low-skilled occupations** are low paying, the costs that these employers save in hiring immigrants are passed along to consumers via a lowered cost of goods and services. According to Ethan Lewis, a professor of economics at Dartmouth College, "The benefits of immigration really come from occupational specialization. Immigrants who are relatively concentrated in less interactive and more manual jobs free up natives to specialize in what they are relatively good at, which are communication-intensive jobs."[25]

Seasonal farm workers pick strawberries in the Salinas Valley of central California. Without immigrant farm workers, the cost of producing food would be considerably higher.

Many immigrants fully embrace their adopted country. They easily adapt to American customs, while also blending their own traditions into the society.

Placing too many restrictions on legal immigration can also lead to a rise in illegal immigration. Since the United States is such a desirable country for people to want to live in, making it harder to come into the country could contribute to people who are desperate for better lives for themselves and their families to come into the country anyway. Since illegal immigrants are less likely to assimilate into the culture and are less likely to pay taxes, a rise in illegal immigration could take a toll on the American economy, while also causing an increase in crime rates.

In addition to providing a significant positive impact on our economy, immigration allows us to build a more diverse society. Immigrants bring their own traditions and customs to this country. As they assimilate into American society they begin to blend those traditions into American life. This enriches the cultural life of America and reflects the notion of America being a great "melting pot." While this process takes time, it enriches our lives and exposes people of all ages and races to new foods, customs, artistic inspiration, and more.

Opening our metaphorical doors to immigrants also improves the image and reputation of the United States of America overseas. By living up to our country's ideals of providing opportunities for people from all over the world, we will gain more respect abroad. From the very beginnings of our country, the United States has welcomed people from all over the world to take advantage of the many opportunities and freedoms that are available here.

Immigrants who have come to this country will help to educate the people that they have left behind about the benefits of being an American citizen or of living in America. Giving more people a taste of what it is like to live as American can only help to improve our image abroad. It makes our nation a safer place to live, as well as upholds the ideals that are expressed in the Pledge of Allegiance, that of a land that provides liberty and justice for all.

The number of positive benefits that legal immigration provides to our economy, society, and culture can't be denied. To place undue restrictions on the numbers of immigrants permitted into the United States would ultimately prove to be detrimental to our economic viability and our relationship with other countries. It would also be against the very ideals that we have claimed as being essential to being American. For these reasons, legal immigration into this country should not be restricted.

A family of Tibetan immigrants celebrate their naturalization at a ceremony outside the home of Thomas Jefferson. The third president was a supporter of immigration.

TEXT-DEPENDENT QUESTIONS

1. What policies against legal immigration has the Trump administration attempted to enact?
2. How do legal immigrants impact employment for American-born workers?
3. In what ways does legal immigration help the economy?
4. How could legal immigrants cause a negative impact on local government and community resources?

RESEARCH PROJECTS

There are conflicting opinions as to whether or not immigrants take jobs away from native-born workers. Using the Internet and your school's library, conduct research on this topic and choose a side. Write persuasive five-paragraph essay on your opinion. Be sure to properly cite your research.

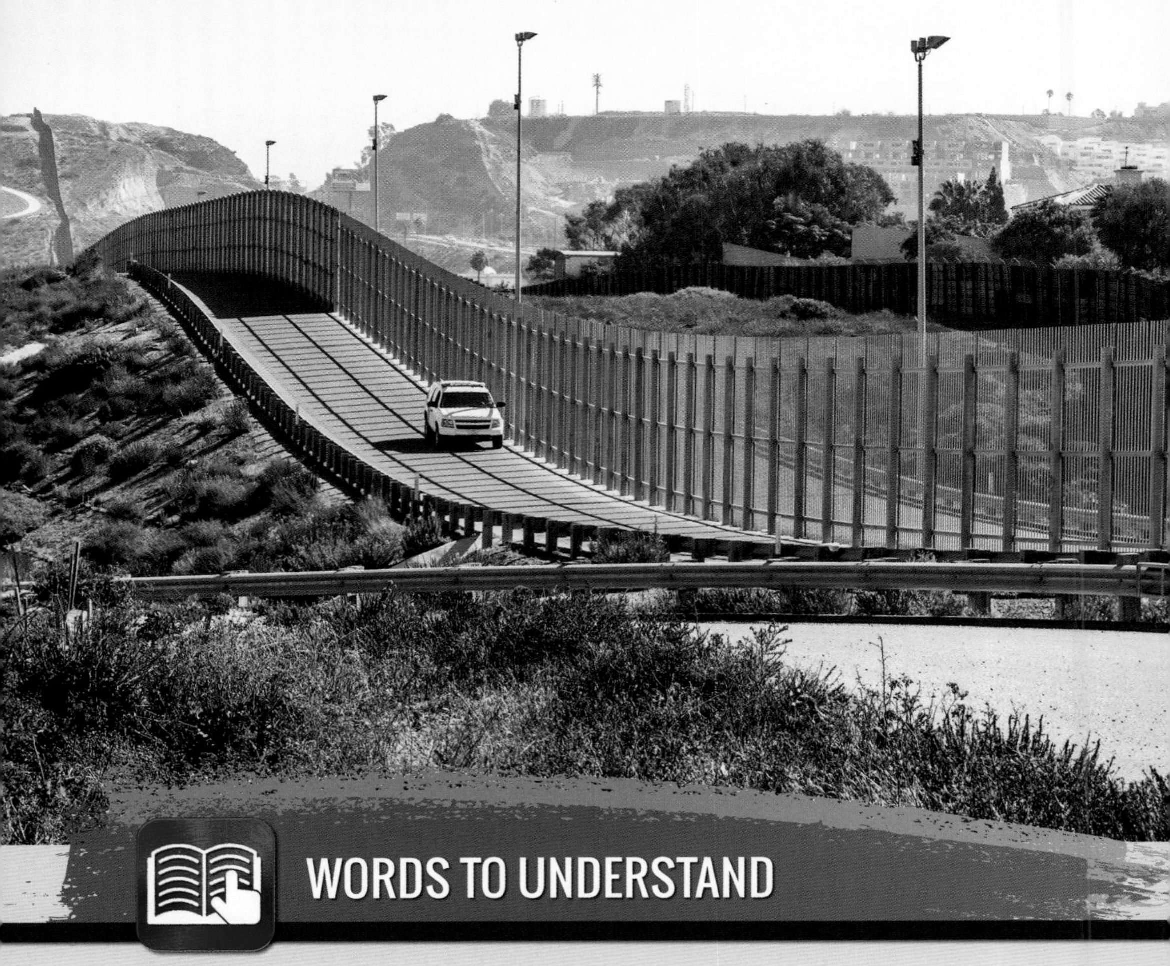

WORDS TO UNDERSTAND

national emergency—a state of emergency proclaimed by a government authority resulting in expanded powers within the government and usually enacted within times of crisis.

bipartisan—a political term used when members of two opposing parties are in agreement on an issue or policy.

illegal immigrants—people who migrate to a country without going through the legal channels available for immigration.

executive powers—the power given to the executive branch of the government (the President) to enforce laws in the United States.

CHAPTER 3

SHOULD THE US BUILD A WALL ON THE SOUTHERN BORDER?

On February 15, 2019, President Donald Trump declared a **national emergency** in order to allocate funds for a wall along the border between the United States and Mexico. The wall has long been a popular issue for Trump. The declaration of a national emergency was made after a **bipartisan** spending bill provided only $1.3 billion for security along the border, far less than the president sought to construct the wall. In order to secure the $5.7 billion in funding that Trump wanted, the president issued an emergency declaration, saying, "We're going to confront the national security crisis on our southern border, and we're going to do it one way or another."[26]

Despite President Trump's insistence on building the wall, more than half of the American people oppose a border wall. A survey conducted by the Pew Research Center in January 2019 found that the "majority of Americans (58 percent) continue to oppose substantially expanding the border wall, while 40 percent favor the proposal."[27] The divide appears to be a political one, with Republicans being more likely to support the wall and Democrats more likely to oppose it.

The reason why President Trump and others desire to build a wall along the border is that they believe that it will deter **illegal immigrants** from entering the United States. The actual number of illegal immigrants is unknown, but the most recent estimates conducted by the Pew Research

BORDER WALL BACKGROUND

While the idea of a border wall has been a hot issue in recent years, it is far from a new solution. The original border wall between the United States and Mexico dates to 1918 when the mayor of Nogales, Mexico, decided to build a fence between his city and the city of Nogales, Arizona. The Arizonans soon built a fence of their own. These were among the first permanent barriers to restrict the movement of people between the United States and Mexico.

By the 1920s, fences were quite common in most border towns. The 1940s saw the United States Immigration and Naturalization Service (INS) start to place barriers along the border. In 1969, President Richard Nixon sent thousands of border agents to the southern border in order to prevent illegal crossings.

During the 1990s, President Bill Clinton began cracking down on illegal immigration by ordering construction of a thirteen-mile-long wall between San Diego and Tijuana. President Clinton also signed

Center as well as federal agencies like the US Census Bureau and the Department of Homeland Security put the figure at between 11 to 12 million unauthorized immigrants.

In addition to the political divide over the border wall, there is also a sharp political divide between Democrats and Republicans over whether or not illegal immigration is an important issue within the United States. As is often the case, the debates around this issue have been both heated

the Illegal Immigration Reform and Responsibility Act. This 1996 legislation increased the penalties for illegal entrants, and also gave the border patrol more funding for patrols and fence construction.

The terrorist attacks of September 11, 2001, caused even more attention to be paid to US borders. Border patrols were increased, and President George W. Bush signed the Secure Fence Act in 2006. This legislation authorized construction of about 700 miles of new border fencing. Over the next few years, more than 600 miles of fences and vehicle barriers were built. In 2011, President Barack Obama cut funding for the rest of the "wall" that had been proposed via the Secure Fence Act. The Obama administration said the cost was too high.

In 2015, presidential candidate Donald Trump repeatedly promised to build a wall between the Mexico and the United States if he were elected. After being elected in November 2016, President Trump continued to promise that a wall would be constructed.

and ongoing. This is evidenced by the fact that many politicians have vowed to block President Trump's declaration of emergency, as they believe that it is an overreach of his **executive powers**. Some of these concerns come from members of the Republican Party. Senator Marco Rubio stated, "We have a crisis at our southern border, but no crisis justifies violating the Constitution."[28] In addition to the opposition in Congress, a number of lawsuits are expected against the declaration.

No matter what the outcome of the President's declaration of a national emergency will be, the debate over the effectiveness of a wall on the Southern border of the United States will likely continue for quite some time. The following short essays detail some of the concerns on both sides of the issue.

Demonstrators in San Francisco protest against Donald Trump's 2019 declaration of a national emergency at the border.

THE US SHOULD BUILD A BORDER WALL

In 2018, there were approximately 467,000 immigrants who were caught attempting to cross the southern border into the United States illegally. These 467,000 people would have joined the estimated 5.4 million illegal immigrants from Mexico who are already in the United States. According to the Pew Research Center, many of these illegal immigrants "make up at least 75 percent of the total unauthorized immigrant population in five states. This is the case in New Mexico (91 percent), Idaho (79 percent), Arizona (78 percent), Oklahoma (78 percent), and Wyoming (77 percent)."[29] Illegal immigrants from Mexico also make up about 69 percent of the illegal immigrant population in the state of California. These illegal immigrants pose a threat to the national security of the United States. They also threaten the economic security of the American citizens. A wall built along the border of the United States and Mexico is the best way to prevent illegal immigrants from coming into the country.

A wall along the southern border will ultimately have a positive impact on the national security of the United States. Currently, the border of the United States and Mexico serves as an entry point for not only illegal immigrants and their families, but also is a source of smuggling and trafficking of both drugs and human beings. "The motivation is reducing infiltration by cartels, gangs, drugs, and human trafficking. Individuals can climb ladders, but it slows them down and limits what they can carry. Vehicles cannot breach the wall, so any truck with weapons, drugs, sex slaves, or worse has to stop, and the smugglers have to climb ladders with only what they can carry."[30] Even if these smugglers and traffickers were able to get through the wall, they will be unable to carry less with them, meaning less weaponry and drugs that cross the border and make it onto the streets of the United States.

In addition to limiting smuggling and trafficking, the border wall can also reduce the risks of terrorists crossing

Supporters of President Trump's immigration policies show their support at a California rally.

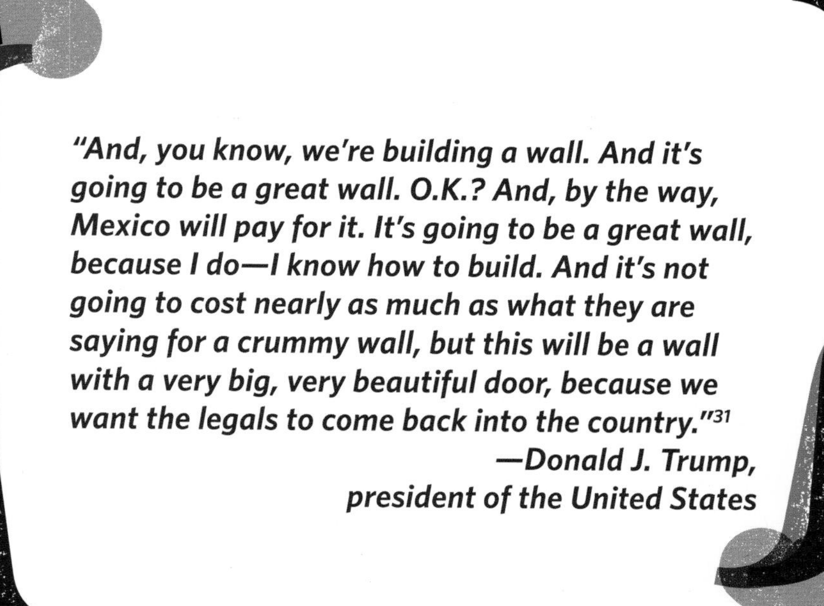

"And, you know, we're building a wall. And it's going to be a great wall. O.K.? And, by the way, Mexico will pay for it. It's going to be a great wall, because I do—I know how to build. And it's not going to cost nearly as much as what they are saying for a crummy wall, but this will be a wall with a very big, very beautiful door, because we want the legals to come back into the country."[31]

—Donald J. Trump, president of the United States

into the United States through the southern border. While there have yet to be any known instances of terrorists utilizing this border to get into the United States, strengthening the border via a wall will allow us to ensure that the country remains protected against this unmitigated potential threat.

There have been demonstrated successes in both deterring and apprehending illegal immigrants in areas of the southern border that already utilize physical barriers. For instance, in the 1990s, nearly 600,000 people tried to cross the border between Mexico and San Diego, California illegally. In 2015, the number had gone down to only 39,000. This is due to both increased border patrols and the addition of a fence along the border. The state of Arizona has also seen some success from physical barriers. Many potential illegal immigrants are apprehended in their attempts to cross the physical barriers present at the Barry M. Goldwater Air Force Range.

Another benefit of constructing a border wall is that the reduction in illegal immigration that will occur due to the

Hondurans traveling through Mexico in a migrant caravan climb into vehicles at dawn to ride to the next stop. This photo was taken in the Mexican state of Oaxaca during November 2018. Such caravans allow thousands of Central Americans to reach the US border, where they request asylum, and are safer than traveling alone through Mexico.

Federal officers arrest a member of the notorious Honduran street gang MS-13 in New York. Preventing illegal immigrants from crossing the border will help to keep criminals out of the country.

wall will save the United States money in the long-term. Illegal immigrants are more likely to have low incomes. These lower incomes place a burden on social services such as health, education, and government assistance programs. Since illegal immigrants are more likely to have lower incomes and are thus more likely to make use of these programs, the burden of cost falls to the middle and upper class American taxpayers. An analysis published by a conservative think tank, the Center for Immigration Studies, found that, "Every new illegal immigrant that enters the United States will cost more than $82,000 each over their lifetime."[32]

Deterring illegal immigrants not only places less of a financial burden on American taxpayers, but it also improves the job market for American citizens and immigrants who have come here legally. While it is difficult to come up with an exact number of how many illegal immigrants are in the workforce, recent studies estimate that around 8 million illegal immigrants are working in the United States. Illegal immigrants are more likely to accept lower wages, making them an attractive option for employers over native-born Americans. While it is against the law to hire illegal immigrants, many employers are able to get around the law by accepting fake documents in order to employ them. Reducing the influx of illegal immigrants willing to accept these wages will encourage employers to increase their wages so that American workers will fill those jobs.

In addition to deterring illegal immigration, a border wall would also send an important message to those around the world who may seek to enter the country illegally, as well as to those employers who currently hire illegal immigrants. According to columnist Robert J. Samuelson, "The wall would symbolize a major shift in US immigration policy—a tougher attitude—that would deter some from crossing the border illegally and, more important, justify legislation requiring employers to verify workers' immigration status before hiring them. If we were to increase border security but not require proof of legal status, much of the wall's benefit would be lost."[33]

It is essential that the border be protected in order to ensure that the people legally residing in the United States are both physically and economically secure. A border wall is the best solution to the growing problem of illegal immigrants crossing over into the United States from Mexico.

A section of the existing border wall in Arizona. The more than 600 miles of barriers that currently exist have significantly reduced illegal border crossings.

THE US SHOULD NOT BUILD A BORDER WALL

The area of the state of Texas that borders Mexico is a stronghold for Trump supporters. Although the Texans who live in this area agree with many of the president's policies, many of them do not agree with his proposed border wall. In fact, a poll conducted by Texas Lyceum in 2018 showed that 61 percent of Texans opposed the border wall. "Trump has done some good things with immigration, but he's 100 percent wrong about the wall," says Dob Cunningham, a rancher and former Border Patrol agent who lives on the border. "I haven't found anybody—and I know people from Nogales [Arizona] to Brownsville—who wants that wall."[34]

The views of Texans like Mr. Cunningham reflect that of the views of Americans as a whole. A survey conducted by the Pew Research Center shows that approximately 58 percent of Americans oppose the building of a border wall. There are many reasons behind the opposition to a border wall. These reasons include the fact that it is not an economically sound plan, that it will do nothing to prevent illegal immigrants from entering the country, that it will have long-lasting consequences on the environment, and that it will tarnish the image and values of the United States. Simply put, constructing a wall along the southern border of the United States and Mexico is not an appropriate or an effective solution to illegal immigration.

One of the biggest arguments against the border wall is its cost. According to an estimate from the Massachusetts

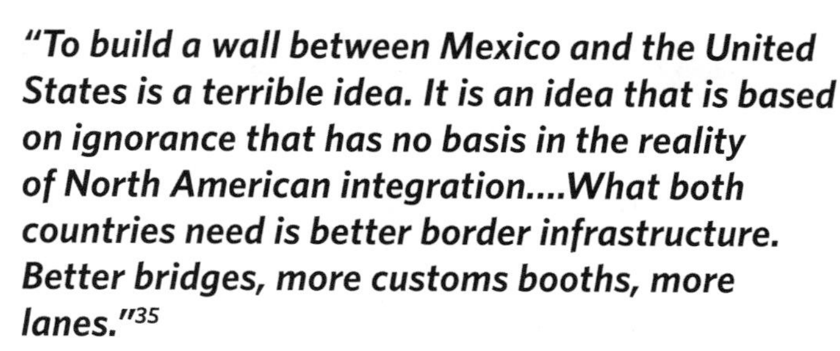

"To build a wall between Mexico and the United States is a terrible idea. It is an idea that is based on ignorance that has no basis in the reality of North American integration....What both countries need is better border infrastructure. Better bridges, more customs booths, more lanes."[35]

—Dr. Luis Videgray, Mexican secretary of Finance and Public Credit

Institute of Technology, "For the full 1,000 miles, Trump's 30-foot wall (with a 10-foot tunnel barrier) would cost \$31.2 billion, or \$31.2 million per mile."[36] These costs only cover the initial construction of the wall and do not take into account the amount necessary to properly maintain the wall in the future. While President Trump has stated that Mexico will be paying for the wall, Mexican leaders have retorted that their country will not be paying for it. It is more likely that American taxpayers will be required to pay the costs of the wall—both for its construction and for future maintenance.

In addition to being expensive to build and maintain, the border wall is no guarantee against illegal immigrants entering the country. Those who are determined to enter

Additional walls would do little to prevent illegal immigration, because most unauthorized immigrants did not sneak across the border. Instead, they were originally admitted legally with a work permit or tourist visa, but did not leave when their authorization to be in the US expired.

the United States illegally will be able to get past the wall whether it is by climbing over it or digging tunnels underneath it. In addition, illegal immigrants crossing over from Mexico can easily arrive within the United States via boat. In 2017, the Editorial Board of the *Los Angeles Times* wrote, "Trump's silly wall can't possibly address much of the problem he seeks to fix....Trump has milked the melodrama of a border wall, but he ignores the likelihood that it would be ineffectual at stopping people from entering the country without permission. Human migration routes are like rivers: If they hit an obstacle, the flow finds a way around it."[37]

A border wall would also fail to eliminate a major source of illegal immigration: that of the immigrant who first arrives in the United States legally and then continues to stay within the country after his or her visa has expired. According to the Pew Research Center, immigrants overstaying their visas made up more than half of illegal immigrants residing within the United States.

In addition being both costly and ineffective, the border wall could also have a negative impact on the environment. For instance, the area of land that encompasses the border is host to several wildlife refuges. The area itself also plays an essential role in migration patterns for a variety of different species. According to wildlife biologist Jeff Corwin:

> If this border wall actually happens, it will be an environmental catastrophe. Essentially, what it's doing is cutting through nature's bridge, which connects Central America to North America and South America. Wildlife have been using this natural corridor for millions of years. And, essentially, what this administration wants to do is put a twelve-hundred mile long barrier right through it. Think of all the different species and creatures that migrate for resources, for reproduction, for seasonality...It would be absolutely devastating. There are over a hundred bird species that migrate that will be critically impacted by this. And there are nearly 90 endangered and threatened species, some of which could very well be pushed to extinction because of this proposed wall.[38]

Many biologists and environmentalists share Corwin's opinion on the environmental impact that the wall would have. The wall could also lead to an increase in flooding as it has in Arizona where approximately 700 miles of fencing was placed. These fences exacerbated flooding during Arizona's rainy season, causing millions of dollars in damage.

Another reason why a border wall should not be built on the border is that a wall goes against the values and ideals of the United States. The United States of America has heralded itself as an open and accepting nation that keeps its doors open for those looking for a better life. To build a literal wall on the southern border goes against this message of freedom and hope. To ignore this message would tarnish the reputation of the United States abroad. It would also negatively impact the relationship that the United States has with Mexico.

A border wall will not be able to fix the issue of illegal immigration and will ultimately wind up being a huge expense for the American government and taxpayers. Instead of wasting money and effort on a system of prevention that is highly ineffective, the United States should pursue other ways to discourage and prevent illegal immigration.

To see how the border wall would negatively impact the environment, scan here.

TEXT-DEPENDENT QUESTIONS

1. In what ways would a border wall harm both the environment and area wildlife?
2. Which states have the highest percentage of illegal immigrants from Mexico?
3. How would a border wall help with national security?
4. In what ways could a potential unauthorized immigrant get around the border wall?

RESEARCH PROJECTS

The idea of a border wall isn't unique to the United States. There have been many border walls constructed throughout history. The most famous of these include the Great Wall of China, the Berlin Wall, the Great Wall of Gorgan, the Belfast Peace Walls, and Hadrian's Wall. Using the Internet, research one of these famous walls. Then create a Powerpoint Presentation that discusses whether or not the wall was effective in protecting the borders of the country in which it was located. Present your findings to your class.

WORDS TO UNDERSTAND

amnesty—the process by which the government forgives illegal immigration and assists an immigrant in becoming a legal resident or citizen of the United States.

demographics—statistics that relate to a particular group or population.

deportations—the forcible removal of people from a country, particularly the removal of those who are there illegally.

CHAPTER 4

SHOULD ILLEGAL IMMIGRANTS HAVE A PATH TO US CITIZENSHIP?

Most estimates of the number of undocumented immigrants residing in the United States say that there are approximately 11 million people here illegally. While the majority of politicians and citizens agree that this is a problem, opinions on what to do over the issue of **amnesty** for undocumented immigrants are divided. A number of solutions have been brought forward to address the problem. These solutions range from mass deportations to allowing some path to citizenship or permanent residency for those who are already here illegally.

According to a survey conducted by the Pew Research Center in 2015, 74 percent of Americans said that there should be a way for illegal immigrants to stay within the United States legally. Generally speaking, this position is held by both Republicans and Democrats, with Republicans being more likely to support citizenship for undocumented immigrants as long as they meet certain requirements such as having a background check, paying fines, and paying taxes.

As with most other political issues, the issue of amnesty has been argued for quite some time. Legislation regarding the issue includes the Immigration Reform and Control Act of 1986. Matthew Spalding, director of the B. Kenneth Simon Center for American Studies at the Heritage Foundation, explains amnesty and the Immigration Reform and Control Act of 1986 in this way:

> In the context of immigration, amnesty is commonly defined as granting legal status to a group of individuals unlawfully present in a country. Amnesty provides a simple, powerful, and undeniable benefit to the recipient: it overlooks the alien's illegal entry and ongoing illegal presence and creates a new legal status that allows the recipient to live and work in the country. The textbook example of such an amnesty is the Immigration Reform and Control Act of 1986. The act's core provision gave amnesty to those who could establish that they had resided illegally in the United States continuously for five years by granting them temporary resident status, which in 18 months was adjustable to permanent residency, which led to citizenship five years later.[39]

In 2007, the Secure Borders, Economic Opportunity, and Immigration Reform Act was introduced in Congress. This bill would have included funding for barriers and border patrol agents, while also providing a way for current illegal immigrants to become citizens. The bill ultimately failed to pass. Other similar reform acts were introduced and also failed to pass in recent years.

Despite the inability of immigration reform acts to pass, Americans seem to have developed some sympathy for undocumented immigrants. A 2018 study by Pew Research Center found that, "The share of Americans who express sympathy for immigrants in the US illegally has remained fairly steady in recent years. Currently, 69 percent say they are very sympathetic (27 percent) or somewhat sympathet-

Demonstrators in Austin, Texas, protest against the federal government policy of separating the families of immigrants caught crossing the border illegally. Parents are sent to jail and prosecuted, while children are placed in custody of the Office of Refugee Resettlement, a federal government agency.

ic (42 percent) toward immigrants in the US illegally."[40]

This public sympathy towards illegal immigrants could be part of the reason why efforts towards granting them citizenship have continued to gain support from politicians on both sides of the political spectrum. It may also be part of the reason why the Development, Relief, and Education for Alien Minors Act (DREAM) and the Deferred Action for

THE DREAM ACT

The DREAM Act is a proposed piece of bipartisan legislation that would allow children whose parents brought them into the United States illegally a pathway to permanent residency and eventually to US citizenship. While the Act has had considerable public support, Congress did not pass the legislation.

First introduced in 2001, the piece of legislation would have allowed qualifying undocumented high-school graduates and GED holders to utilize three steps towards US citizenship by going to college, the armed services, or work. Qualifying undocumented immigrants must also be of good character, meaning that they must be obeying US laws.

The first step of the process would allow any undocumented immigrant who was brought into

Children Arrivals (DACA) have garnered so much public support.

As sympathetic attitudes towards undocumented immigrants continue to grow, it is apparent that some solution will have to be found. While perceptions and support for illegal immigrants have changed significantly across all **demographics**, those in younger demographics are more likely to have a positive view of them. This trend indicates that it is important to have a thorough understanding of both sides of the debate. The following short essays explore the arguments for and against granting citizenship to illegal immigrants residing within the United States.

the United States while under the age of 15 to receive conditional permanent residence (CPR) for eight years. Once this status has been maintained, lawful permanent residence (LPR) can be granted. To receive this status, an individual must have completed at two years of college, been in the military for at least two years, or have been employed for three years. After being on LPR status for five years, an individual can then become a United States citizen.

If it is ever enacted, the DREAM Act would allow young Americans who have lived in the United States for most of their lives to obtain legal status as American citizens. Since they were brought here as children, their status as illegals is not their fault, hence the popular support amongst Americans for the passage of the law.

ILLEGAL IMMIGRANTS SHOULD HAVE A PATH TO CITIZENSHIP

In 1986, President Ronald Reagan signed the Immigration Reform and Control Act (IRCA). While the act itself strengthened immigration enforcement and penalized employers who hired illegal immigrants, it also offered a path for those who had resided in the country for five or more years. This amnesty was offered to immigrants who met certain conditions to apply for temporary legal status. After a period of time, they could then apply for permanent legal status. Eventually, these same once illegal immigrants could apply for citizenship to the United States. Due to this, the IRCA became the first widespread legalization program in the United States. Its legacy continues today and has inspired other efforts at reforming current immigration policies in a way that can bring legal status to more undocumented immigrants. In order to carry on the work of this important piece of legislation, it is imperative that the United States grants citizenship to illegal immigrants.

A benefit of regularizing the status of illegal immigrants is that it will have a positive impact on the economy of the United States. A report published by the Center for American Progress in 2013 found that legalizing undocumented immigrants leads to higher wages for the previously illegal immigrants. Earning more money means they will be paying more tax dollars into the system. It also leads to less of a burden on government and social services aimed towards those with low incomes. "As our study demonstrates, legal

> ***"We have to deal with the 11 million individuals who are here illegally...We've got to lay out a path—a process that includes passing a background check, paying taxes, paying a penalty, learning English, and then going to the back of the line, behind all the folks who are trying to come here legally.... So that means it won't be a quick process but it will be a fair process. And it will lift these individuals out of the shadows and give them a chance to earn their way to a green card and eventually to citizenship."[41]***
>
> ***—Barack Obama***

status and a road map to citizenship for the unauthorized will bring about significant economic gains in terms of growth, earnings, tax revenues, and jobs—all of which will not occur in the absence of immigration reform or with reform that creates a permanent sub-citizen class of residents," write study authors Robert Lynch and Patrick Oakford. "We also show that the timing of reform matters: The sooner we provide legal status and citizenship, the greater the economic benefits are for the nation."[42]

In addition to being beneficial to the economy, legalizing undocumented immigrants could have a positive impact on national security. In most proposals for legalizing undocumented immigrants, thorough vetting of the immigrant in

A demonstration outside the White House in support of the Deferred Action for Childhood Arrivals program, 2017. Although DACA expired in March 2018, federal courts have ruled that DACA protections will continue until a new program is implemented.

question is required. This vetting process consists of background checks to ensure that only those without criminal or questionable backgrounds will be given legal status. This system will also reward those who may be here illegally, but who despite that fact are living law abiding lives and making positive contributions to their communities.

Going in hand in hand with the positive impact on national security is that granting illegal immigrants legal status can help to make the country safer by making communities a safer place to live. Many illegal immigrants are reluctant to cooperate with law enforcement agencies for fear of being sent back to their home countries. Regularizing their status will make them more likely to work with law enforcement in order to create safer communities.

Granting illegal immigrants amnesty can also lower crime rates. When illegal immigrants are kept out of the job market due to their illegal status, or are trapped in low-income jobs, they are more likely to commit crimes. By giving them a clear road to citizenship, the United States can reduce the number of immigrants who turn to crime. Paolo Pinotti, a professor at Bocconi University, states, "These people are not bad. They're not evil people or anything. It's just that they have the wrong incentives. If they're not allowed to work in the official economy, sooner or later they end up committing crimes."[43]

Many people who are opposed to providing amnesty for undocumented immigrants suggest that they should be deported back to their home countries. This is an unrealistic expectation due to the large numbers of immigrants currently residing in the United States illegally. As President Barack Obama said during the 2016 presidential election campaign, "The notion that we're gonna deport 11, 12 million people from this country—first of all, I have no idea where Mr. Trump thinks the money's gonna come from. It would cost us hundreds of billions of dollars to execute that."[44]

In addition to being extremely expensive, mass **deportations** would also pose a number of logistical problems. For instance, there would need to be places where large numbers of illegal immigrants could be held while awaiting deportation. There is also the question of what to do with undocumented immigrants whose children were born in the United States, and are therefore legal US citizens. Taking these parents away from their children would not only prove to be traumatic for the families, but could also tarnish America's reputation overseas.

Providing an easier path to citizenship for undocumented immigrants isn't just economically and socially beneficial to the United States. It is also the humane, compassionate, and moral thing to do. America has long prided itself in being a place where anyone can move to in order to live a life full of freedom and opportunity. To deny this to those immigrants who may have initially come here illegally but who are otherwise living productive lives within their communities goes against the American ideals and visions of a land full of opportunity. That is why we the United States should offer citizenship or legal residency to illegal immigrants.

ILLEGAL IMMIGRANTS SHOULD NOT RECEIVE CITIZENSHIP

In 2013, the Border Security, Economic Opportunity and Immigration Modernization Act was brought to the floor of the US Senate. This bill would have made it easier for many undocumented immigrants to become citizens of the United States. While the bill was not passed, it sparked a tremendous amount of debate over the issue of granting citizenship to illegal immigrants. James Sensenbrenner, a Republican congressman from Wisconsin, had this to say about the proposed bill: "Extending amnesty to those who came here illegally or overstayed their visas dissuades people from joining the nearly 4.5 million would-be Americans who are following the rules. This creates economic problems, national security concerns, and a human rights crisis as immigrants risk death crossing into America."[45]

Sensenbrenner was correct in his assessment. Granting citizenship to undocumented immigrants is not the appropriate path for the United States to take when it comes to dealing with the problem of illegal immigrants.

As Sensenbrenner pointed out, it would be exceptionally unfair to the millions of people waiting to immigrant legally to the United States if America were to grant citizenship to those who decided to enter the country illegally. The time and resources spent on providing amnesty to illegal immigrants could be better used by helping those trying to enter the United States legally, many of whom are seeking to immigrate to America due to the unsafe nature of their home countries.

Another reason why illegal immigrants should not be granted amnesty is that it would place a great burden on the economy of the United States. While it is true that former illegal immigrants would probably pay more in taxes, the fact of the matter is that many of these immigrants are low-wage earners who will be more likely to utilize government benefits once they become eligible for them as legal residents or citizens. Due to their low levels of education and skills, as well as their inability to speak English, these undocumented immigrants will most likely not be able to move out of the sort of low-wage jobs that they took while still in the United States illegally. Kristen Williamson from the Federation for American Immigration Reform (FAIR)

Scan here for reasons why amnesty isn't a good approach.

US Border Patrol agents in Texas process foreigners who were caught trying to cross the US border illegally. Detaining and deporting illegal immigrants costs American taxpayers millions of dollars each year.

says, "This is a largely low-skill, low-wage population that would now be required to file taxes, but would not necessarily be people who are paying net contributions to taxes, so they would be eligible for benefits."[46] This would place yet another burden on American taxpayers, as well as on an already overburdened welfare system. A study published by the Center for Immigration Studies found that, "The total net cost of the IRCA amnesty after ten years comes to over $78 billion."[47]

Allowing illegal immigrants to stay within the United States is also far more expensive than deporting them would be. According to another study conducted by the Center for Immigration Studies, "Illegal immigrants are a large net fiscal drain....Deportation, on the other hand, is not that costly relative to the fiscal costs illegal immigrants create."[48] This study showed that in 2016, a deportation cost $10,854 per removal. Meanwhile, the lifetime cost of

Border Patrol agents search migrants caught illegally crossing the border near California's Imperial Valley.

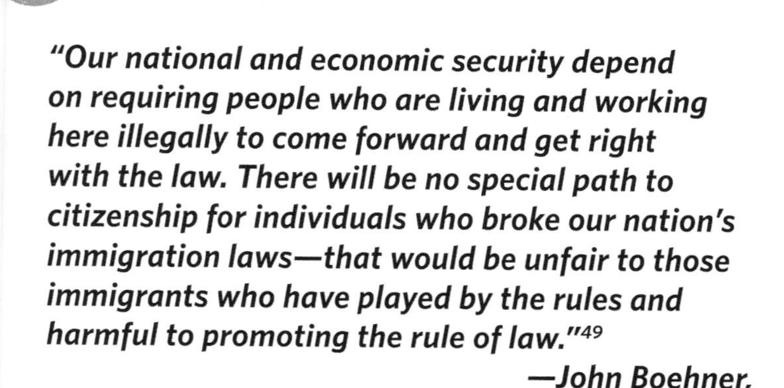

"Our national and economic security depend on requiring people who are living and working here illegally to come forward and get right with the law. There will be no special path to citizenship for individuals who broke our nation's immigration laws—that would be unfair to those immigrants who have played by the rules and harmful to promoting the rule of law."[49]

—John Boehner, former speaker of the US House of Representatives

allowing an illegal immigrant to stay within the United States was estimated at $65,292 per illegal immigrant.

Immigrants who arrive here illegally are also more likely to become involved in criminal activities. US Immigration and Customs Enforcement (ICE) reports that there were 105,140 illegal immigrants arrested in 2018 who were previously convicted criminals. In addition to that, a study conducted by the Crime Prevention Resource center found that, "Undocumented immigrants are at least 142 percent more likely to be convicted of a crime than other Arizonans."[50] This same study also stated, "Young convicts are especially likely to be undocumented immigrants....Even after adjusting for the fact that young people commit crime at higher rates, young undocumented immigrants commit crime at twice the rate of young US citizens. These undocumented immigrants also tend to commit more serious crimes."[51]

Allowing undocumented immigrants to be eligible for legal resident status or citizenship could also lead to more illegal immigrants entering the United States. For instance, the Immigration Reform and Control Act of 1986 lowered the illegal immigrant population in the short term, but was followed in the 1990s by a huge increase in illegal immigration. There were roughly 3.2 million illegal immigrants in the United States before that legislation was passed in 1986. Although many of them took advantage of the opportunity to become legal, millions more crossed the border illegally. By 2007, the illegal immigrant population reached a new peak of over 12 million people. The lesson is that providing amnesty will lead to more illegal immigrants, who hoping to receive amnesty themselves without having to wait in line.

Amnesty for undocumented immigrants is an unfair policy that also contributes to a decrease in safety and economic security for the United States. In the words of Peter Skerry, a professor of Political Science at Claremont McKenna College, "Amnesty is a bad idea both as policy and as politics."[52]

TEXT-DEPENDENT QUESTIONS

1. According to the Pew Research Center, what is the percentage of Americans who support granting citizenship to undocumented immigrants?
2. What was one of the unintended consequences of the Immigration Reform and Control Act of 1986?
3. Why is mass deportation an unrealistic means of getting illegal immigrants out of the country?
4. What are three reasons why amnesty for illegal immigrants is a bad idea for the United States?

RESEARCH PROJECTS

There are political lobbies for every political issue imaginable. Research a pro-immigration reform lobby such as the Federation for American Immigration Reform or the Center for Immigration Studies. Write a two-page paper on how effective the organization is.

WORDS TO UNDERSTAND

universal language—a language that is understood by the majority of people around the world.

socioeconomic—the interaction that happens between social and economic factors within groups of people.

proficiency—possessing a high level of skill in a subject.

green cards—documents issued by the United States government that allows immigrants to legally live and work on a permanent basis within the United States.

CHAPTER 5

SHOULD IMMIGRANTS BE REQUIRED TO LEARN ENGLISH?

The debate over whether or not immigrants to the United States should be required to learn English has been an ongoing one, reaching far back into the history of the country. The nation's second president, John Adams, believed that all Americans should speak English, as English was destined to become a **universal language** like Latin once was. Adams once wrote, "English is destined to be, in the next and succeeding centuries, more generally the language of the world than Latin was in the last or French is in the present age. The reason of this is obvious, because the increasing population in America and their universal connection and correspondence with all nations will, aided by the influence of England in the world, whether great or small, force their language into the general use, in spite of all the obstacles that may be thrown in their way, if any such there should be."[53]

While President Adams was in favor of the English language, it is important to note that the Founding Fathers never established a national language. Due to America's origins as English colonies, the need to establish a national language never came up. Because most of the people residing in the colonies spoke English, the business of the new nation was conducted in English. However, the Founding

WHAT'S IN A NAME?

While the United States has welcomed waves of immigrants onto its shores, many of these immigrants have experienced hostility directed towards them until they became fully assimilated into American society. This hostility was often worst during periods where the United States experienced mass immigration. Between 1850 and 1913, the borders of the United States were open and approximately 30 million immigrants came to the United States, mostly from Europe. Due to nativist hostility, it was necessary for immigrants from Ireland, Italy, Russia, and eastern Europe to assimilate into American life quickly. This was accomplished by adopting American cultural practices and language.

Another way that immigrants assimilated into the surrounding culture was by giving their children American-sounding names. According to a study conducted by the Stanford Institute for Economic Policy Research, "having an American-sounding name was a badge of assimilation that conferred genuine economic and social benefits....Children with less-foreign-sounding names completed more years of

Fathers had no way of predicting the influx of immigrants that would begin flooding the country throughout the course of its history. The question of whether or not they should be required to learn English in order to be granted legal immigrant status or citizenship has continued to be debated by politicians and native-born citizens alike.

schooling, earned more, and were less likely to be unemployed than their counterparts whose names sounded more foreign. In addition, they were less likely to marry someone born abroad or with a foreign-sounding name."[54]

The adoption of American names indicates that an immigrant population has become fully integrated into the fabric and society of life in the United States. It shows that a sense of belonging was important to these immigrants and their families. It also shows that a growing sense of identification with America and other Americans became important to these immigrants. The fact that millions of immigrants have historically assimilated into American society shows that fears about immigrants being unable to become fully American are, and always have been, misplaced. As the authors of the Stanford study wrote, "The evidence is clear that assimilation is real and measurable, that over time immigrant populations come to resemble natives, and that new generations form distinct identities as Americans."[55]

As of 2016, a little more than half of the immigrants living in the United States were proficient English speakers, according to the Pew Research Center. Pew's survey also found that 35 percent of immigrants reported that they spoke English very well, while 16 percent stated that they only spoke English at home. Contrasted with the fact that 72 percent of native-born Americans believe that immigrants should learn to speak English when they move to the United States, it is easy to see how this particular issue has become a heated one.

The essays that follow explore both sides of the question as to whether or not learning English should be required of all immigrants who desire to reside within the United States.

To learn more about the debate on whether immigrants to the US should learn English, scan here.

IMMIGRANTS SHOULD BE REQUIRED TO LEARN ENGLISH

According to a survey conducted by the Gallup Organization in 2013, "72 percent of Americans say it is essential that immigrants living in the United States learn to speak English."[56] This belief reflects the opinions of many important political and social figures in both the present and the past. It also clashes with the fact that the US Census found that almost 20 million immigrants have limited **proficiency** with the English language. There are a number of reasons why these immigrants should be required

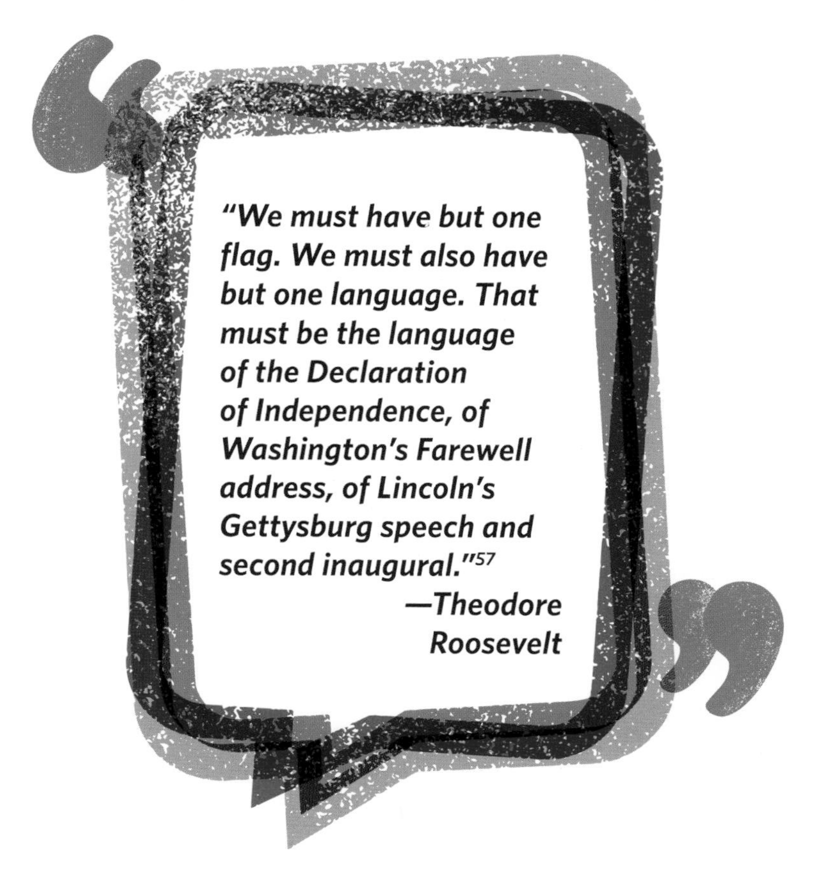

to learn English if they desire to live here legally and/or become citizens.

There is no denying the fact that English is the primary language of the United States. In order for immigrants to function within American society, they will need to be able to communicate in the predominant language. This is one of the underlying factors behind Senator Marco Rubio's 2013 proposal for an amendment to the failed Border Security, Economic Opportunity, and Immigration Modernization Act. As journalist Ray Suarez for PBS News Hour explained, "Florida Republican Marco Rubio has proposed an amendment requiring immigrants to be proficient in English and pass a civics test. Under current law, only applicants for US citizenship, not those applying for **green cards**, must prove English proficiency."[58]

Abraham Morales, a Hispanic insights specialist with a communications firm agreed with Senator Rubio's proposed amendment. In an opinion piece for *The Denver Post*, Morales wrote:

> I believe all new immigrants should learn English. I am one of the 40 million immigrants living in this country and, after more than a dozen years here, I am still learning new vocabulary and idiomatic expressions every day. Learning how to speak and write English helps us not only to survive, but to advance as well. I know of talented new citizens whose level of English limits their ability to pursue career opportunities, to be more engaged in their children's education, or to better understand complex US systems such as health care.[59]

The data supports Mr. Morales's personal experiences. According to the Migration Policy Institute, immigrants

Expecting immigrants to the United States to assimilate into society is not a new idea. In this photo from the 1920s, immigrants in the Detroit area learn English and study the US political system as part of a naturalization class.

with Limited English Proficiency (LEP) rates "were more likely to live in poverty than English-proficient individuals."[60]

In addition to helping immigrants to survive life in the United States, learning English can also help them to become better assimilated into American society. Speaking English helps immigrants to feel like they are a part of society, as a shared language promotes cohesiveness within groups. This sense of cohesiveness will help immigrants to feel as if they are a part of the communities in which

Immigrants who learn English and embrace American culture and values are more likely to feel accepted and be successful.

they live. Being able to speak English proficiently will also provide immigrants with a tie to American history and culture. This tie will hopefully be passed along to future generations. As President Ronald Reagan wrote in 1987, "By emphasizing the importance of a common language, we safeguard a proud legacy and help to ensure that America's future will be as great as her past."[61]

Failing to learn English can also lead to immigrants becoming socially isolated. This isolation is for both immigrants and for native-born American citizens. As immigrants isolate themselves due to not knowing the predominant language within a country, it becomes more likely that the native-born residents of that country will begin to resent and fear them. Requiring that immigrants learn English can help to eliminate this sense of a foreign entity "taking over" a native-born citizen's country.

Columnist Sean Kennedy writes, "It threatens social cohesion as immigrants become socially isolated from the mainstream and resentment boils up that an influx of non-English-speaking people is upending traditional American customs. The ties that bind the 'little platoons' of society together grow frayed and break in ugly ways."[62]

In order to ensure the success of immigrants to the country, it is imperative that they be required to learn the predominant language. In the United States, this language is English. By making a requirement that legal immigrants learn English, the United States will help immigrants to America achieve economic and social success.

IMMIGRANTS SHOULD NOT BE REQUIRED TO LEARN ENGLISH

The United States has been referred to as a great "melting pot" since the 1780s. While the term originated during this time period, it did not become popular until late mid-to-late nineteenth century. The term itself refers to the blending of immigrants from many different countries and cultures into one singular American culture.

The vision behind this great melting pot is not one that requires that immigrants to the United States should be expected to give up their culture, traditions, or their language in order to be fully accepted as residents or citizens. Establishing legal requirements that immigrants will need to learn English goes against the very idea of what the American experience is. Therefore, immigrants to the United States should not be required to learn English in order to legally reside here.

While English is the predominant language, there has never been a designated official language within the United States. As Abi Hunter, a high school student from Albuquerque, New Mexico, writes, "The United States is a multilingual nation. Most large American cities have burgeoning immigrant communities from all over the globe, and even smaller ones, such as mine, have signs and official documents translated into one, two, or even three languages."[63]

In fact, from the very beginnings of the United States there have been accommodations made for people who aren't proficient in English. An example of this is that sev-

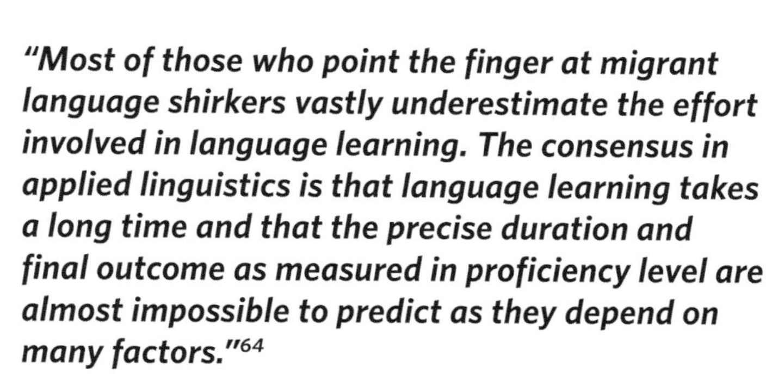

"Most of those who point the finger at migrant language shirkers vastly underestimate the effort involved in language learning. The consensus in applied linguistics is that language learning takes a long time and that the precise duration and final outcome as measured in proficiency level are almost impossible to predict as they depend on many factors."[64]

—Ingrid Piller, linguistics professor

eral of the documents that were drafted during the Continental Congress between the years of 1774 and 1789 were translated into French and German. English was certainly the primary language of most colonists, but the Founding Fathers believed that it was not the place of a democratic government to dictate what language people could or should speak.

Another reason why immigrants should not be required to learn English is that classes to learn English can be expensive. Many immigrants who come to this country would be unable to afford these classes. Finding the time to go to class could be problematic as well, as could acquiring childcare in order to attend the classes. In addition to

Businesses and restaurants use multiple languages to promote their businesses in a Korean neighborhood in Manhattan.

this, there are not enough classes available for immigrants to take in order to learn how to speak English. According to Barbara Mujica from Georgetown University, "I think one of the problems that we're facing right now is that we don't have enough classes available. We don't have enough classes available. We're telling people that they have to learn English, but we really have to provide the mechanism by which they would learn English."[65]

A requirement to learn English also doesn't take into account the fact that learning another language is a difficult task. It's also a task that takes some people longer than others to accomplish. According to Ingrid Piller, a professor of applied linguistics at Macquarie University in Sydney, Australia, "Most people readily forget that it takes about twelve years to learn your first language. The first five or six years from birth are devoted to acquiring oral fluency and then another six years or so are needed to learn how to read and write, to acquire the academic and textual conventions of a language and also to extend grammatical structures, expand vocabulary and refine pragmatic conventions."[66] Professor Piller also states that it can take up to 10,000 hours of study to become proficient in a second language.

Requirements to learn English often do not allow for differences in how quickly individuals learn. Factors that contribute towards someone's ability to learn a second language include age, prior education, gender, **socioeconomic** status, race, religion, and sheer luck. A legal requirement to learn a language will not be able to factor in these differences, and would therefore prove to be an immense hardship to those who simply want to move to America in order to have better lives.

Additionally, demands that immigrants learn English aren't realistic. If a legal requirement is set for immigrants to learn English, how will it be determined whether or not a person has made enough progress in the eyes of the law? There is no real way to determine whether or not someone has learned enough English in the necessary timeframe.

Finally, learning another language is not something that can be forced. The desire, motivation, and the right set of circumstances have to be present in order for anyone to learn a second language. The decision as to whether or not he or she should learn English is one that should be made by the immigrant, not by the government.

As the immigrant population within the United States continues to grow, it is important that American policy makers understand how important it is that immigrants are not required to learn English in order to reside in the country. The obstacles that a language requirement would pose on these immigrants could deter them from coming to the country, or it could cause undue hardship on the immigrant and his or her family. While it is important that immigrants be encouraged to learn English, establishing a legal requirement would be completely counterproductive and ineffective.

TEXT-DEPENDENT QUESTIONS

1. What are some of the factors that determine someone's ability to learn a new language?
2. How does proficiency in the English language benefit immigrants?
3. Is there a legally designated official language within the United States?
4. What does the "melting pot" refer to?

RESEARCH PROJECTS

Using the Internet and the library, conduct research on the challenges that immigrants face when it comes to learning a second language. Form your own opinion as to whether or not it is feasible to require immigrants to speak English before they can be granted residency or citizenship of the United States. Then write a one-page persuasive paper explaining your views.

SERIES GLOSSARY OF KEY TERMS

affidavit—a sworn statement, in writing, that sets out a person's testimony.

affirmative action programs—programs that are intended to improve the educational or employment opportunities of members of minority groups and women.

BCE and CE—alternatives to the traditional Western designation of calendar eras, which used the birth of Jesus as a dividing line. BCE stands for "Before the Common Era," and is equivalent to BC ("Before Christ"). Dates labeled CE, or "Common Era," are equivalent to Anno Domini (AD, or "the Year of Our Lord").

colony—a country or region ruled by another country.

democracy—a country in which the people can vote to choose those who govern them.

discrimination—prejudiced outlook, action, or treatment, often in a negative way.

detention center—a place where people claiming asylum and refugee status are held while their case is investigated.

ethnic cleansing—an attempt to rid a country or region of a particular ethnic group. The term was first used to describe the attempt by Serb nationalists to rid Bosnia of Muslims.

felony—a serious crime; in the United States, a felony is any crime for which the punishment is more than one year in prison or the death penalty.

fundamentalist—beliefs based on a strict biblical or scriptural interpretation of religious law.

median—In statistics, the number that falls in the center of a group, meaning half the numbers are higher than the number and half are lower.

minority—a part of a population different from the majority in some characteristics and often subjected to differential treatment.

paranoia—a mental disorder characterized by the strong belief that the person is being unfairly persecuted.

parole—releasing someone sentenced to prison before the full sentence is served, granted for good behavior.

plaintiff—a person making a complaint in a legal case in civil court.

pro bono—a Latin phrase meaning "for the public good," referring to legal work undertaken without payment or at a reduced fee as a public service.

racial profiling—projecting the characteristics of a few people onto the entire population of a group; for example, when police officers stop people on suspicion of criminal activity solely because of their race.

racism—discrimination against a particular group of people based solely on their racial background.

segregation—the separation or isolation of a race, class, or group from others in society. This can include restricting areas in which members of the race, class, or group can live; placing barriers to social interaction; separate educational facilities; or other discriminatory means.

ORGANIZATIONS TO CONTACT

American Economic Association
2014 Broad Suite 305
Nashville, TN 37203
Phone: (615) 322-2595
Fax: (615) 343-7590
Website: https://www.aeaweb.org

Center for Immigration Studies
1629 K Street N.W., Suite 600
Washington, D.C., 20006
Phone: (202) 466-8185
Fax: (202) 466-8076
Website: https://cis.org

Fair Immigration Reform Movement
Phone: (202) 339-9330
Email: jnazarett@communitychange.org
Website: https://fairimmigration.org

Federation for American Immigration Reform (FAIR)
25 Massachusetts Ave. N.W., Suite 330
Washington D.C. 20001
Phone: (877) 627-3247
Fax: (202) 387-3447
Email: dray@fairus.org
Website: http://www.fairus.org

Immigration Advocates Network
Email: support@immigrationadvocates.org
Website: www.immigrationadvocates.org

Migration Policy Institute
1400 16th Street N.W., Suite 300
Washington, D.C. 20036
Phone: (202) 266-1940
Website: info@migrationpolicy.org

US Citizenship and Immigration Services
Phone: (800) 375-5283
Website: https://www.uscis.gov

US Department of Homeland Security
Secretary of Homeland Security
Washington, D.C., 20528
Phone: (202) 282-8495
Email: DHSSecretary@hq.dhs.gov
Website: https://www.dhs.gov

US Immigration and Customs Enforcement
500 12th St., SW
Washington, D.C. 20536
Phone: (202) 732-0104
Email: ICE-FOIA@dhs.gov
Website: https://www.ice.gov

FURTHER READING / INTERNET RESOURCES

FURTHER READING

Cannato, Vincent J. *American Passage: The History of Ellis Island*. New York: Harper Perennial, 2010.

Hayworth, J.D. *Whatever It Takes: Illegal Immigration, Border Security, and the War on Terror*. Washington, DC: Regnery Publishing, 2006.

Krikorian, Mark. *The New Case Against Immigration: Both Legal and Illegal*. New York: Penguin, 2008.

Osborne, Linda Barret. *This Land Is Our Land: A History of American Immigration*. New York: Abrams, 2016.

Vasic, Ivan. *The Immigration Handbook: A Practical Guide to United States Visas, Permanent Residency and Citizenship*. Jefferson, NC: McFarland & Company, 2008.

INTERNET RESOURCES

http://www.pewresearch.org
The website for the Pew Research Center. This site provides data on a number of political and social issues, including legal and illegal immigration.

https://cis.org
This is the website for the Center for Immigration Studies. It contains a number of studies and publications that provide more information on the impact of immigration on the United States.

https://www.usa.gov/immigration-and-citizenship
The official website of the United States. It offers some basic information on immigration and citizenship.

https://www.ilrc.org
The website of the Immigrant Legal Resource Center. Links to articles and other publications on the topic of immigration are available.

https://www.migrationpolicy.org
Official website of the Migration Policy Institute. There are links to articles and studies that further detail important issues within immigration.

CHAPTER NOTES

[1] Emma Lazarus, "The New Colossus," Statue of Liberty National Monument New York (accessed on February 27, 2019). https://www.nps.gov/stli/learn/historyculture/colossus.htm

[2] Israel Zangwill, *The Melting Pot* (New York: The American Jewish Book Company, 1921). https://www.gutenberg.org/files/23893/23893-h/23893-h.htm

[3] Thomas Paine, "Common Sense" (February 14, 1776). http://www.gutenberg.org/ebooks/147

[4] George Washington, letter to Reverend Francis Adrian Vanderkemp (May 28, 1788) Accessed via http://teachingamericanhistory.org/library/document/letter-to-reverend-francis-adrian-vanderkemp/

[5] Ellis Island Foundation, "Immigration Timeline," The Statue of Liberty-Ellis Island Foundation, Inc. (accessed on February 25, 2019). https://www.libertyellisfoundation.org/immigration-timeline

[6] Ohio History Central, "Know-Nothing Party," Ohio History Connection (accessed on February 28, 2019). http://www.ohiohistorycentral.org/w/Know-Nothing_Party

[7] Lorraine Boissoneault, "How the 19th-Century Know Nothing Party Reshaped American Politics," *Smithsonian* (January 26, 2017). https://www.smithsonianmag.com/history/immigrants-conspiracies-and-secret-society-launched-american-nativism-180961915/

[8] Harry S. Truman, "Special Message to the Congress on Admission of Displaced Persons," Harry S. Truman Presidential Library and Musuem (July 7, 1947). https://trumanlibrary.org/publicpapers/index.php?pid=1947

[9] Ronald Reagan, quoted in "Ronald Regan's Shining City of Exceptional Immigrants," *Forbes Magazine* (December 2, 2013). https://www.forbes.com/sites/stevenhayward/2013/12/06/ronald-reagans-shining-city-of-exceptional-immigrants/#53564920639f

[10] Charles Hirschman, "The Impact of Immigration on American Society," Eurozine (May 11, 2017). https://www.eurozine.com/the-impact-of-immigration-on-american-society/

[11] Hirschman, "The Impact of Immigration on American Society."

[12] Stephen Miller, quoted in "The Outrage Over Family Separation Is Exactly What Stephen Miller Wants," *The Atlantic* (June 19, 2018). https://www.theatlantic.com/politics/archive/2018/06/stephen-miller-family-separation/563132/

[13] Benjamin Franklin, "Observations Concerning the Increase of Mankind and the Peopling of Countries," Federation for American Immigration Reform. http://www.fairus.org/issue/legal-immigration/quotes-historical-figures

[14] Thomas Jefferson, "Letter to Hugh White, Esq," *The Writings of Thomas Jefferson* (Washington, DC: Taylor and Maury, 1854), p. 894.

CHAPTER NOTES

[15] Alan Gomez, "All the Ways President Trump Is Cutting Legal Immigration," *USA Today* (June 12, 2018). https://www.usatoday.com/story/news/world/2018/06/12/donald-trump-cutting-legal-immigration/692447002/

[16] Kim S. Reuben and Sarah Gault, "What Do Immigrants Cost State and Local Governments?" Urban Wire (June 5, 2017). https://www.urban.org/urban-wire/what-do-immigrants-cost-state-and-local-governments

[17] Calvin Coolidge, "Accepting the Republican Presidential Nomination," Calvin Coolidge Presidential Foundation (August 14, 1924). https://www.coolidgefoundation.org/quote/quotations-i/

[18] Steven A. Camarota, "National Security," Center for Immigration Studies (Accessed February 20, 2019). https://cis.org/Immigration-Topic/National-Security

[19] Amy L. Wax and Jason Richwine, "Low-Skill Immigration: A Case for Restriction," *American Affairs Journal* (Winter 2017). https://americanaffairsjournal.org/2017/11/low-skill-immigration-case-restriction/

[20] Gal Ariely, "Globalization, Immigration and National Identity: How the Level of Globalization Affects the Relations Between Nationalism, Constructive Patriotism and Attitudes Toward Immigrant," *Group Processes Intergroup Relations* (December 19, 2011). http://www.academia.edu/12992689/Globalization_immigration_and_national_identity_How_the_level_of_globalization_affects_the_relations_between_nationalism_constructive_patriotism_and_attitudes_toward_immigrants

[21] Dick Armey, "From Letter to a Constituent," Federation for American Immigration Reform (September 22, 1995). https://fairus.org/issue/quotes-contemporary-public-officials

[22] Doug Bandow, "Immigration Benefits the US, So Let's Legalize All Work," *Forbes Magazine* (September 16, 2013). https://www.forbes.com/sites/dougbandow/2013/09/16/immigration-benefits-the-u-s-so-lets-legalize-all-work/#156ae3fe4d12

[23] Benjamin Fearnow, "Immigrants Account for Two-Thirds of US Economic Growth Since 2011, Analysis Finds," *Newsweek* (September 9, 2018). https://www.newsweek.com/migrants-immigration-1113006

[24] Ian Goldin, quoted in Fearnow, "Immigrants Account for Two-Thirds of US Economic Growth Since 2011, Analysis Finds."

[25] Ethan Lewis, quoted in "The Danger From Low-Skilled Immigrants: Not Having Them," *The New York Times* (August 8, 2017). https://www.nytimes.com/2017/08/08/business/economy/immigrants-skills-economy-jobs.html

[26] Donald Trump, quoted in "Donald Trump Declares National Emergency to Free Up Billions of Dollars for Border Wall," *USA Today* (February 15, 2019). https://www.usatoday.com/story/news/politics/2019/02/15/government-shutdown-trump-declare-emergency-get-wall-funding/2859532002/

[27] Pew Research Center, "Most Border Wall Opponents, Supporters Say Shutdown Conces-

sions are Unacceptable," Pew Research Center (January 16, 2019). http://www.people-press.org/2019/01/16/most-border-wall-opponents-supporters-say-shutdown-concessions-are-unacceptable/

[28] Marco Rubio, quoted in "Trump Declared a National Emergency Over a Border Wall. What Happens Next?" *USA Today* (February 16, 2019). https://www.usatoday.com/story/news/politics/2019/02/16/donald-trump-national-emergency-border-wall-fight/2876668002/

[29] Ana Gonzalez-Barrera and Jean Manuel Krogstad, "What We Know About Illegal Immigration from Mexico," Pew Research Center (December 3, 2018). http://www.pewresearch.org/fact-tank/2018/12/03/what-we-know-about-illegal-immigration-from-mexico/

[30] Benjamin R. Dierker, "3 Benefits Of A Border Wall That No One Is Talking About," *The Federalist* (June 20, 2018). http://thefederalist.com/2018/06/20/3-benefits-border-wall-no-one-talking/

[31] Donald Trump, "Face the Nation Transcript," CBS News (August 23, 2015). https://www.cbsnews.com/news/face-the-nation-transcripts-august-23-2015-trump-christie-cruz/

[32] Barnini Chakraborty, "Each Illegal Immigrant Costs US $82G, Conservative Think Tank Claims," Fox News (January 9, 2019). https://www.foxnews.com/us/each-illegal-immigrant-cost-us-82k-conservative-think-tank-claims

[33] Robert J. Samuelson, "Yes, Build the Wall!" *The Chicago Tribune* (October 11, 2017). https://www.chicagotribune.com/news/opinion/commentary/ct-perspec-wall-daca-immigration-trump-samuelson-1012-20171011-story.html

[34] Dob Cunningham, quoted in "Wall of Contention," *The Star-Telegram* (May 24, 2017). https://www.star-telegram.com/news/state/texas/article152402734.html

[35] Luis Videgaray Caso, PhD, quoted in "Mexico Won't Pay for Trump's Wall, Treasury Secretary Says," CNN (March 3, 2016). https://www.cnn.com/2016/03/03/politics/mexico-treasury-secretary-trump-wall/index.html

[36] David Bier, "Why the Wall Won't Work," *Reason* (May 2017). https://www.cato.org/publications/commentary/why-wall-wont-work

[37] The Times Editorial Board, "Pretty Much the Only Thing Trump's Border Wall Will Block Is Common Sense," *Los Angeles Times* (March 25, 2017). https://www.latimes.com/opinion/editorials/la-ed-trump-immigration-border-wall-mexico-20170325-story.html

[38] Jeff Corwin, quoted in "Trump's Border Wall 'Catastrophic' for Environment, Endangered Species: Activists," NBC News (April 22, 2017). https://www.nbcnews.com/science/environment/trump-s-border-wall-catastrophic-environment-endangered-species-activists-n748446

[39] Matthew Spalding, "Undeniably Amnesty: The Cornerstone of the Senate's Immigration Proposal," The Heritage Foundation (June 25, 2007). https://www.heritage.org/immigration/report/undeniably-amnesty-the-cornerstone-the-senates-immigrationproposal

[40] Pew Research Center, "Shifting Public Views on Legal Immigration Into the US" Pew Research Center (June 28. 2018). http://www.people-press.org/2018/06/28/shifting-public-views-on-legal-immigration-into-the-u-s/

[41] Barack Obama, "Remarks by the President on Comprehensive Immigration Reform," The White House: President Barack Obama (January 29, 2013). https://obamawhitehouse.archives.gov/the-press-office/2013/01/29/remarks-president-comprehensive-immigration-reform

[42] Robert Lynch & Patrick Oakford, "The Economic Effects of Granting Legal Status and Citizenship to Undocumented Immigrants," Center for American Progress (March 20, 2013). https://www.americanprogress.org/issues/immigration/reports/2013/03/20/57351/the-economic-effects-of-granting-legal-status-and-citizenship-to-undocumented-immigrants/

[43] Paolo Pinotti, quoted in "Will Legalizing More Immigrants Reduce Crime?" American Economic Association (January 25, 2017). https://www.aeaweb.org/research/legalizing-immigrants-impact-crime-rate

[44] Barack Obama, quoted in "Obama Calls Trump's Plan to Deport Illegal Immigrants Unrealistic," Reuters (November 12, 2015). https://www.reuters.com/article/usa-election-obama-immigration/obama-calls-trumps-plan-to-deport-illegal-immigrants-unrealistic-abc-idUSL1N13803Z20151113

[45] James Sensenbrenner, quoted in "Sensenbrenner: The Senate's Amnesty Echoes Only Failure," *The Washington Times* (July 1, 2013). https://www.washingtontimes.com/news/2013/jul/1/the-senates-amnesty-echoes-only-failure/

[46] Kristen Williamson, quoted in "Immigration Reform? Good or Bad for the Economy?" CNBC Markets (February 11, 2013). https://www.cnbc.com/id/100449802

[47] Federation for American Immigration Reform, "Why Amnesty Isn't the Solution," FAIR (August 2007). http://fairus.org/issue/amnesty/why-amnesty-isnt-solution

[48] Steven A. Camarota, "Deportation vs. the Cost of Letting Illegal Immigrants Stay," Center for Immigration Studies (August 3, 2017). https://cis.org/Report/Deportation-vs-Cost-Letting-Illegal-Immigrants-Stay

[49] John Boehner, quoted in "Standards for Immigration Reform," *Wall Street Journal* (January 30, 2014). https://blogs.wsj.com/washwire/2014/01/30/house-republicans-release-standards-on-immigration-overhaul/

[50] John R. Lott, "Undocumented Immigrants, US Citizens, and Convicted Criminals in Arizona," SSRN (February 10, 2018). https://papers.ssrn.com/sol3/papers.cfm? abstract_id=3099992

[51] Lott, "Undocumented Immigrants, US Citizens, and Convicted Criminals in Arizona."

[52] Peter Skerry, "Why Amnesty Is the Wrong Way to Go," The Brookings Institution (August 12, 2001). https://www.brookings.edu/opinions/why-amnesty-is-the-wrong-way-to-go/

[53] John Adams, quoted in "Do You Speak American?" PBS: From Sea to Shining Sea (Accessed on February 25, 2019). https://www.pbs.org/speak/seatosea/officialamerican/johnadams/

[54] Stanford Institute for Economic Policy Research, "What History Tells Us About Assimilation of Immigrants," Stanford Public Policy Program (accessed on February 22, 2019). https://publicpolicy.stanford.edu/news/what-history-tells-us-about-assimilation-immigrants

[55] Stanford Institute for Economic Policy Research, "What History Tells Us About Assimilation of Immigrants."

[56] Jeffrey M. Jones, "Most in the US Say It's Essential That Immigrants Learn English," Gallup Organization (August 9, 2013). https://news.gallup.com/poll/163895/say-essential-immigrants-learn-english.aspx

[57] Theodore Roosevelt, quoted in "Should English Be the Law?" *The Atlantic* (April 1997). https://www.theatlantic.com/magazine/archive/1997/04/should-english-be-the-law/376825/

[58] Ray Suarez, quoted in "Should Immigrants Be Required to Learn English?" PBS News Hour (June 21, 2013). https://www.pbs.org/newshour/show/should-immigrants-be-required-to-learn-english

[59] Abraham Morales, "Learning English Can Help Immigrants Survive," *The Denver Post* (March 8, 2013). https://www.denverpost.com/2013/03/08/learning-english-can-help-immigrants-survive/

[60] Jie Zong & Jeanne Batalova, "The Limited English Proficient Population in the United States," The Migration Policy Institute (July 8, 2015). https://www.migrationpolicy.org/article/limited-english-proficient-population-united-states

[61] Ronald Reagan, quoted in Sean Kennedy, "Learning English Should Be Part Of American Experience," CNN (September 17, 2015). https://www.cnn.com/2015/09/17/opinions/kennedy-english-language-immigration/index.html

[62] Sean Kennedy, "Learning English Should Be Part of American Experience."

[63] Abi Hunter, "'Speak English Or Get Out?'" HuffPost (July 23, 2013). https://www.huffingtonpost.com/abi-hunter/foreign-languages_b_3325252.html

[64] Ingrid Piller, "The Real Problem With Linguistic Shirkers," Language on the Move (March 30, 2016). http://www.languageonthemove.com/the-real-problem-with-linguistic-shirkers/

[65] Barbara Mujica, quoted in "Should Immigrants Be Required to Learn English?"

[66] Piller, "The Real Problem With Linguistic Shirkers."

INDEX

INDEX

AUTHOR'S BIOGRAPHY AND CREDITS

ABOUT THE AUTHOR

Heather Pidcock-Reed holds a Master's Degree in Professional Writing from Chatham University, where she studied topics such as science & environmental writing, political & news writing, technical writing, teaching technical writing, and writing for digital media. She also holds a BFA from the Academy of Art University in Motion Pictures & Television with an emphasis in Screenwriting. Heather's main interests lie in education, journalism, and writing for digital media. She currently resides in La Junta, Colorado.

PICTURE CREDITS

© 3000ad | Dreamstime.com: 74; © Richard Gunion | Dreamstime.com: 66; © Marcio Silva | Dreamstime.com: 40; © Sherry V. Smith | Dreamstime.com: 48; © Joe Sohm | Dreamstime.com: 46, 92; Everett Historical: 8, 10, 12, 91; Immigration and Customs Enforcement Photo: 57; Library of Congress: 6, 16, 18; used under license from Shutterstock, Inc.: 35, 36, 59; Ryan Rodrick Beiler / Shutterstock.com: 44; Sheila Fitzgerald / Shutterstock.com: 2, 52; Vic Hinterlang / Shutterstock.com: 56, 69; Iodrakon / Shutterstock.com: 39; Mike Ledray / Shutterstock.com: 54; David Litman / Shutterstock.com: 43; Christian Mueller / Shutterstock.com: 96; Christopher Penler / Shutterstock.com: 23; Christine Ruddy / Shutterstock.com: 84; Rena Schild / Shutterstock.com: 26; Steven Sullivan / Shutterstock.com: 1; US Customs and Border Protection: 62, 79, 80; US Customs and Immigration Services: 29; US Department of Justice: 32.